BUT AS FOR ME

The Question of Election in the Life of God's People Today

BUT AS FOR ME

by

ANDRÉ LACOCQUE

John Knox Press
ATLANTA

Unless otherwise indicated, the Scripture quotations in this book are
from the Revised Standard Version Bible, copyright 1946, 1952, and ©
1957, 1971, 1973 by the Division of Christian Education, National Council of the Churches of Christ in the U. S. A., and are used by permission.

Scripture quotations accompanied by the letters "TEV" are from *Good
News Bible: The Bible in Today's English Version,* © 1966, 1971, 1976
by the American Bible Society, and are used by permission.

Scripture quotations accompanied by the letters "KJV" are from the
King James Version of the Holy Bible.

Library of Congress Cataloging in Publication Data

Lacocque, André.
  But as for me.

  Includes bibliographical references.
  1. Election (Theology) I. Title.
BT810.L32   234   78-71042
ISBN 0-8042-1172-8

© 1979 John Knox Press

Printed in the United States of America

For Claire, my wife,
Michel, Pierre-Emmanuel, and Elisabeth,
and their families present and to come,
I have written this book
as if it were my last.

Acknowledgments

It is my pleasure to express my gratitude to several persons whose work has made the publication of this book possible. First of all, my student Douglas C. Runnels, Ph.D., has read and edited my manuscript with commendable care and understanding. His numerous suggestions have been precious challenges for me.

I also thank the Chicago Theological Seminary for generously putting its secretarial staff at my disposal, in particular the late Miss Dorothy I. McFarlane and her unflagging willingness to serve with unequaled love, and her successor, Miss Carol Eck, whose patience and efficaciousness are most gratifying.

Contents

BUT AS FOR ME

1. | The Identity of Israel

We do not have anything we could offer them [the Jews]. But what they offer us excels us . . . only the miscarried Jew is like us . . . the ordinary person is an unfulfilled Jew.[1]

What does it mean that God calls us to be his own? This question lies behind the whole history of the Biblical literature, for, from one perspective, it was written in various times as God's people struggled to respond to this enigma and to understand it. In the present attempt to answer this question, I will look at the historical meaning of Israel's chosenness.

In the light of Israel's self-consciousness, one interpretation can be dismissed immediately. Election is not on the part of God a mere declaration of intention not followed by real actualization or incarnation, nor is it an external quality adding itself, through whatever extraordinary process, to the innate or natural human qualities. Election does not *add* anything to a panoply of virtues, congenital or acquired. On the contrary, according to Biblical testimony the "chosen Israel" is a wholistic reality, a "Gestalt" as we say today. There is no Israel facing her election; nor is there, so to speak, an election in quest of someone to be elected. There is only Israel *as* elected, or an election *as* applied to God's people. In the experience of Israel it is a *transforming* power permeating the community, thereby changing Abram to Abraham, Jacob to Israel. Capable of operating in people, world, and history, God's grace is a creative power manifesting itself in the movement from chaos to order (Gen. 1:2–3).

This particular self-understanding, one can argue, falls in

line with the very experience which created Israel as a people
in the first place. For "Israel" is hardly an ethnic label; it is the
name of a movement, a process, a becoming. It is the name of
the transfiguration of Jacob (Gen. 32:28) and, hence, not so
much a result as a pointing forward to a future fulfillment.
Rudolf Bultmann speaks of the "inner connection between indicative and imperative, namely, that the indicative is the
ground of the imperative."[2] Israel in this perspective is a
"given" which needs to be realized. The prophets do not use
the word "Israel" indifferently (cf. the alternating expressions
"sons of Israel" and "house of Jacob" in Amos 3:12ff.; 4:5, 12; 5:1,
2, 3, 4; 6:15). In like manner, the land of Israel which is promised, given, and granted by God, must be painfully conquered
by its people. In other words, while election is an ontological
reality, it is not a status. Just as we are, each of us, what we do,
according to our individual primordial choice, Israel's self-
realization stems from her existential will to be chosen.

In this sense, it is imperative for the prophet to call his
people to become what they really are, and to confront them
with the "impossible possibility" of being rejected and forsaken
by God (cf. Hos. 1:9). How often indeed did Israel experience
her condemnation as uttered by her own prophets, sent, as she
had later to confess, by God for the sake of justice and truth! No
nation has been more severely chastened; none has been more
frequently disciplined.

Paradoxically, it is this tension between actual election and
possible rejection that maintains Israel in her role of incarnating
a Choice. Because the one who is *Ruḥama,* "pitied," or *'Ammi,*
"my people," makes herself *Lo-ruḥama,* "not pitied," and *Lo-
'ammi,* "not my people" (Hos. 1:6, 8), she is condemned,
purified, and saved. As Luther once said daringly to Melanch-
thon, *"Pecca fortiter!"* (Make your sins more substantial!)

In what follows, I shall assume the unity of God's people
from Abraham until today. For, on the one hand, the very
foundation of the covenantal relationship is the affirmation by

God of fidelity to his promises (cf. Rom. 9:4). And, on the other hand, the unity of Israel reflects the very nature of the living God (cf. Gen. 1:26–27; Lev. 11:44; 19:2).

True, Israel's identity has been a problem to herself as well as to others. For more than thirty-three centuries, the sociological and historical uniqueness of the children of Abraham has remained a mystery. When did Israel become "Israel"? What led a group of clans and tribes with particular traditions of their own to unite as one people and accept a common destiny? In fact, the problem is extremely complex. The scholarly consensus is that there simply was no such thing as a single Israelite people sharing a unified history, ethics, philosophy, language, and theology. If we accept the reconstruction of the German historian of the Bible Martin Noth, for example, the origin of the entity called Israel is to be traced back to several sources, forming several streams which eventually united in one river. The traditions were as diverse as the different peoples who federated around a common sanctuary (alternately Shiloh, Gilgal, Shechem, Bethel) into a group of tribes or an amphictyony. However, the passing of time and the common experiences of history diminished the main differences among them. As a result, a consolidated faith which we could call Yahwistic orthodoxy finally emerged after the exile in Babylon. It gave us the Biblical documents, fully revised and corrected, as we know them today.

This very valuable contribution of scholarship is welcome. It helps us to recognize the diversity within ancient Israel and her Scriptures. Neither the former nor the latter appeared suddenly in history as a finished product; so Israel's identity is seen as a dynamic rather than a static reality. But while the plurality of peoples and documents (sometimes even gods) in the Bible has been noticed by many critics, there has been little attention given to the forces which proved capable of unifying such diverse elements. Surely, however, it is not enough to retrace (with Albrecht Alt, for example)[3] the process of absorption by "Yhwh" of deities locally worshiped by farmers and other settled people. What tremendous force was at work capable of such a grand unification without contamination with "Canaanism"? What force was capable of creating such a strong although elusive identity of the people of Israel? Strong it was and is, for it has triumphed over incredible odds for thirty-three centuries or so. Elusive? Yes again, for scholarship is incapable of bringing forth any convincing single definition of it. So much so that one can wonder whether there has ever been anything like one "Israel" in historical reality! Perhaps the word covers a utopian concept pertaining to fantasy rather than any concrete historical entity! From whatever angle one considers the identity of Israel, it seems that one is doomed to become ensnared in a myth conceived by the wishful imaginations of a band of dreamers (priests, prophets, or rabbis), a myth which has nothing to do with the actual Israel of old or with the contemporary situation of the Jews. To be sure, this does not mean that the dream or the myth was not fruitful and worthwhile. On the contrary, once that problem is put in brackets, as it were, the sky seems suddenly cleared of its clouds! The procedure may be cheap but it is comfortable. Isn't it what in the past many have done who read an "Old Testament" as a disincarnated piece of literature? Those who indulge in such a mythologizing process divorce the Scriptures from their authors and natural recipients. The Bible is no longer Jewish. Israel's universalism is used against her: there is no Israel left in the picture, only the "nations." Paradoxical as this may look, it is nevertheless what happens in many popular Christian milieux, and even in some scholarly quarters so much fascinated by single trees that they overlook the forest. In other words, singled-out Biblical "spiritual statements" or respectively analytically sorted-out religious phenomena become the center of scrutiny or piety, but the people of Israel, the real authors and the real recipients of their Scriptures, are forgotten on the way.

It is indispensable, however, to realize that before any text was written, before anything worthy of being orally transmitted ever existed, Israel was. And after all transmission, oral and written, Israel continues to be. The Scriptures are an artistic achievement, like a painting or a poem. The unity of the composition is grounded ultimately in the unity and the uniqueness of the composer. The great architect and visionary is Israel.[4]

A scholarly approach which does not struggle with the creative genius by which Israel was able to transform the raw material provided by neighboring nations into an original ("demythologized" say the scholars), genuine, and unique product is surely incomplete. It does not tell us about the energy capable of welding a "mixed multitude" (Exod. 12:38; Num. 11:4) into a community of faith and history. A man's biography which would content itself with a list of the extremely diverse events, phenomena, options, philosophies, reactions, and responses in the subject under examination would fail finally to see behind and within the phenomena, the man himself. So it is with Israel. Paradoxically, sharp criticism of the sacred texts and the conclusion that "Israel" is a historical impossibility pays the greatest possible tribute to the fundamental reality and unity of Israel. Just as a living person remains beyond the grasp of scientific formulas, so also Israel's existence presents a unity which analysis can only begin to comprehend.

Today Israel appears to us as an impenetrable mystery. But, after all, has not this mystery persisted since the beginning? There is no more reason for asking what entitles the Jews to claim to be Israel today than there is reason to wonder what provided the historical continuity between the community of Zerubbabel in the fifth century B.C.E. and the people under Solomon in the tenth century B.C.E. Between Zerubbabel and Solomon every imaginable constitutive element of the Israelite identity had changed (with one exception which will be specified later). Moreover, there were by Zerubbabel's time many more Jews living abroad than in Palestine; and, though they looked toward Jerusalem as the center of their existence, they had their own peculiar conceptions, their own teaching, and even their own sense of identity. By what right could they claim membership in the house of "Israel"?

Again, on what ground can a people claim to remain faithful to itself? What legitimatizes Americans' claim to be Abraham Lincoln's heirs? The only answer is history, common destiny.

The problem would be similar for an individual: what makes a fifty-year-old man the same person (despite profound differences) he was at the age of fifteen? Existentialism and psychoanalysis have taught the answer: the choice to assume his history. In a decisive way, to claim is to proclaim one's readiness to be measured by the standards of one's identity. In the case of the Jews, more than of any people, these standards are also those of the past; for it is for them a matter of faith that the fidelity and the steadfastness of God's acts in the past gave to the Hebrews' history its unity and made of "a mixed multitude" (Exod. 12:38), of a "rabble" (Num. 11:4), the *verus Israel* (St. Augustine's phrase).

To recapitulate then, Biblical scholarship has administered the *coup de grace* to Biblical fundamentalism in demonstrating that the Scriptures abound in conflicting conceptions, discrepancies, doublets, inconsistencies, schools of thought, theological strata, foreign influences, diversity of provenances and intentions, and sophisticated literary genres as well as folk narratives. The texts are undeniably circumstantial, written in response to the changing needs of a living community. After Hermann Gunkel, modern exegetes must begin their inquiry by looking for those circumstances underlying the writing of a particular text. The first duty is to establish for each Scriptural unit, as clearly as possible, the *Sitz im Leben*—the setting in life, the historical rationale for producing the text in the first place. The placing of a text in the sixth or in the ninth century B.C.E., for example, will have enormous consequences for our understanding of that text, for Israel had other problems and produced different responses during the exile than in the period of the united monarchy in Palestine.

But once this caveat is duly heeded and respected, the question is: what next? Is there, crowning all the theologies represented in the Scriptures, anything like a theology of the Bible? So it seems, at any rate, in regard to the grouping of the "biblia" into one book and its canonization. Was such a move legitimate? Before answering that question, we must first recall that the canonization of the Hebrew Scriptures was a long process in successive stages. The enterprise was no easy task and, certainly, authorities came with mutually exclusive criteria. Those, however, who in Israel took the responsibility for collecting and grouping the great variety of traditional documents were led by a powerful centralizing sentiment. For them the uniqueness of their people was actually mirrored in the infinite diversity of images and conceptions of the texts. Israel, as a vital, living community, was capable, at all stages of her development and growth, of assimilating all the diversities, differences, divergencies, discrepancies. The historical Israel reconciled the irreducible terms of the tension between positive and negative, weakness and strength, despair and hope, sinfulness and sanctity, death and life. For them, in other words, the veritable unifying factor, the only life-giving soul, of the Bible was the historical concrete Israel. With the Scriptures, they have also transmitted to us that legacy.

Now, not all heritages are equally valuable or evenly welcome. It is important, I think, for us to realize once again that the Scriptures have been collected and transmitted by traditionalists who had such a potent conception of the decisive character of their historical community. As impressive as it is, however, it is not necessarily convincing for our contemporaries. Indeed, at this point, some readers may think that the problem of Israel's identity has been further complicated—not clarified. It is still compounded by the question of the relationship between the Israel of old and those who today are known as "Jews" (=Judaeans). What tells us that, measured by the high standards of Biblical Israel, the Jews of today can be considered the continuation of the historical reality bearing that name?

Despite the fact that, in all justice, the problem is reversed —the burden of proof ought to rest upon those who argue the discontinuity between the modern Jews and ancient Israel—the question will not be avoided. But it demands that we first seek the deepest level of Israel's identity; then, and only then, may we consider the extent to which ancient and modern Israel are congruent.

The object of this book is precisely to explore this issue. To do so, I shall scrutinize some selected declarations reflecting Israel's self-consciousness. My method is definitely phenomeno-logical, as will immediately appear in the following chapter on "God's private property." Israel proclaims God her Creator, thus objectifying herself in front of Someone who is forever the "I" of a relationship in which she is his "Thou." Then I will turn to one of the most crucial statements of God, creating *"ex nihilo"* a new identity for Israel now engaged in the covenantal relationship with him. Exodus 19:4–6, already in the back-ground of chapter 2, is further explored in chapters 3 and 4. Israel, private property of God, functions in the world as a kingdom of priests and a holy nation. Such is her *raison d'être* and the only rationale she can discern for God's electing her in the first place. For election is, as I have already stressed, no external status or standing. One is elected *for* a task, a role, a mode of living in the world. Israel had/has the consciousness of being called to the highest possible mission: to be kingly priest in the universe, to be holy and a ferment of holiness in the world, the light of the nations . . . a "Messianic People" (chapter 5).

Once again we thus discover that Israel's problem of identity with which we started our inquiry is inseparable from her prac-tical, existential, dynamic engagement in the process of world existence. Israel is what she does. Israel becomes Israel. Like her land, whose dimension of promise is never canceled even by the people's settlement there, Israel is a benediction to the world in process of fulfillment. This statement is clearly prob-lematic. What is the dialectical relationship between promise and fulfillment? How can a divine promise ever find a historical and human accomplishment? I face this issue in chapter 5 by way of a reflection upon the notion of *failure,* envisaged from a theological point of view. Is accomplishment a synonym of success? Is failure another word for impotence?

This slant allows me, at that point, to introduce in a direct way a partner of Israel in the so-called *Heilsgeschichte* (history of salvation), viz. the Church. She had been constantly in my mind—the reader won't miss that point, I believe. But as historically the people of Israel precedes the advent of the Christian Church, so also in a theological reflection it must be the starting point and, for that matter, must remain the constant reference. There is an Israel without the Church; there is no Church without Israel. Why this is so, and what theological and existential import it has upon Jewish and Christian existence, are the subjects of chapters 6 and 7. Ever since the birth of the Church, and more specifically of a "Christendom," the Western world (i. e., that part which has historically displayed the greatest energy in nearly all human activities) has been the scene of the confrontation of two religions with universalistic pretensions: Judaism and Christianity, or, in terms of their institutionalized manifestations, the Synagogue and the Church (chapter 7). Their dichotomy is time and time again made a scandal and a folly by misunderstandings, misrepresentations, bigotry, to say nothing of sheer hatred and bloodthirst. Is there something more positive to say about and to expect from their duality? Is there a mutuality fertilizing their polarity? Is their togetherness indispensable in the economy of God's salvation act? Such are some of the questions dealt with in chapters 6 and 7.

Finally, I return, in the last chapter, to the problem of identity. For Jesus' question to his disciples, "who do people say I am?" is not exclusively valid as far as the Nazarene is concerned. It is also Israel and the Church's question to the world, yesterday, today, forever.

2. God's Private Property

"You yourselves have seen what I did to the Egyptians, and how I lifted you on eagles' wings and brought you to myself. Now, therefore, if you will hearken to my voice and keep my covenant, you shall be my private property from among all peoples; for all the earth is mine; and you shall be to me a kingdom of priests, and a holy nation." [Exod. 19:4–6, my translation]

Related to the question of identity, Israel has always thought of herself as God's private property. No claim, however, has been harder to make or has caused more tribulation and taken more lives. But Israel's self-identity proceeds from that consciousness that she is chosen, known, loved, by someone else. She conceives herself as *in relationship* and insists that apart from this relationship she has no being. She maintains that there can be no substitute for the way her partner sees her; she can only describe her reflection in her lover's eyes.

The strangeness of Israel's destiny really begins here. Israel has no identity of her own, if by identity we mean the fruits of a Promethean self-achievement. For this reason Israel's claim to chosenness must be carefully distinguished, for example, from the Third Reich Germans' obsession with forging a heroic identity of their own. Such attempts were already old when the Hebrew Scriptures were gathered: " 'Come, let us build ourselves a city, and a tower [let us create a "new order"] with its top in the heavens [something for eternity], and let us make a name for ourselves [let us have some reality in our own eyes, let us escape our vertigo of nothingness], lest we be scattered abroad upon the face of the whole earth [lest we not be distinguished as the "race of lords"].' " (Gen. 11:4) Such a try to escape inner emptiness through violence, the most ludicrous weapon of the weakling, had to clash head-on with its own contradiction, namely the Jews. So history came to its summit: the Third Reich as the nonexistent *par excellence* (in sheer reference to itself) met God's chosen Israel as the existent *par excellence* (in reference to someone else). The one morbidly in love with self tried to crush the beloved of another. Ironically, in attempting to deny the chosenness of Israel, the monster was paying the greatest historical tribute to its reality. It showed that the Jews are *different*. Even the family names represent a difference, for to be called Isaac or Cohen is already the sign of a particular choice. Nobody can approach Israel without having to confront the extraordinary constituents of her personality.

We necessarily step up to an unfamiliar level when reflecting upon Israel. Time and again, non-Jews have felt a strangeness in dealing with her, and more than once this has become an irritation. How dare she be different from us? How dare she be refractory to a logical appraisal of her? Is not the "mystery of Israel" perhaps a disguise for emptiness, or worse for unnameable practices? Can we allow the Jews their otherness? Many, from Martin Luther to Napoleon and Karl Marx, have thought that an appropriate means of persuasion might bring the Jews back into step with everybody else. Paradoxically, however, the notion of chosenness was never abandoned by those Gentile (or Jewish in the case of Marx) theoreticians—it was simply reapplied! The charismatic advocates of Jewish assimilation identified the truly chosen people as the Lutherans, or the French, or the international working class. Chosenness, when not precisely qualified, can be made to apply to virtually any nation or group.

True, "choosing" evades any logical appraisal, as does love or life. But no less than these, election is an event lived by men and women. It does not originate in reason, and yet election is experienced in history, in time. Its motives are irrational—as love is irrational—but its effects are directly accessible. Such a state of affairs is indeed a "mystery"—a reality that saturates daily life but which remains inexplicable in its totality.

The rabbis, directly concerned by the problem, traced the origin of Israel's election back to the creation of the world, that is, to a moment beyond history. In other words, there was for them really no chronological origin for the foundation of Israel's existence. Before Israel was in time, she was already in the mind of God, desired by him, elected as his own. This conception is not merely apologetic; it is an attempt to deal with the impossibility of fixing in time the inception of an artistic creation: it is always *"ex nihilo."*

"In the beginning," before all things, before any ulterior action, before all and beyond all that is to follow, says Genesis 1:1, came the word of election, the declaration of love, God's initiating word which made relationship possible, which created someone with whom to enter into dialogue, someone to bring God out of isolation. It is the prime and the ultimate word of God: the "Thou" which makes possible the "I." God, through his word, through his election of somebody *else,* became a Person. He became a Person-in-relation, for, from Israel's point of view, existence presupposes relationship. As for what God was in the "time" before he related to his creatures and to the universe, it is veiled in mystery and lies beyond our comprehension. He was, says the Zohar, the *Ein Sof,* the positive Nothingness, from which all existence springs. Be that as it may, God's reality as Creator and Redeemer is first achieved when there is a creature, someone to love, to care for, and to redeem. This implies that this creature, through the very status of creature, beloved of the Lover, redeemed of the Redeemer, disposes of an unlimited power: only this creature can acknowledge the reality of God. The partnership initiated by God was, in Israel's eyes, a true relationship. Far from being a confrontation of All with Nothing, both terms of the polarity were, through their very relation to each other, put in a status of need for each other. This is obvious as far as the creature is con-

cerned; "when you take away their breath, they die and return
to their dust. When you send forth your Spirit, they are created;
and you renew the face of the ground." (Ps. 104:29–30, my
translation) But the converse is also paradoxically true—that the
existence of God as Creator and Redeemer depends upon his
creature. And this in fact is *the* condition for the drama of the
rupture between the two lovers. Israel does not speculate on
the potentiality of evil being as it were engrained in the fabric
of creation. But she rightly intuits that there is in the highest
triumph of God, viz., his creation, also the gravest sign of weakness: God *can* be circumvented by his unfaithful partner, for he
is in love, he is love! As soon as "Adam" knew that, i. e., as soon
as he knew God, he had no rest till he tried this omnipotent
weapon against his Creator. Had he not used that power of his
—as the myth describes—he would have wondered forever,
and dreamed of ever more subtle and more sophisticated ways
to kill God. He had to do it, like the sick man dreaming of raping
a woman. But, as in the case of the rapist, the crime does not
quench the desire. Ever since "Adam" (human being) laid a
hand on God, the dream he thought to thus exhaust ceaselessly
recurs. He wonders what went wrong and how to better succeed next time around. I shall take up this point again later; let
me for now return to the primal act of revolt of "Adam."

Paraphrasing Jean-Paul Sartre, one could say: The creation
has turned around against God.[1] "No sooner," says Orestes to
Zeus, "had you created me than I ceased to be yours." God has
put himself in a position to be rejected by his creature. He has
exposed himself to the denial, by his partner, of his very reality.[2]
Of course, a relationship begun on the basis of tyranny on the
part of the divinity would not lend itself to such a failure. In
choosing to relate with someone other than himself, in choosing
to become essentially love (cf. 1 John 4:8; Jonah 4:2), God exposed himself truly and decisively to the approval or refusal of
"Adam."

As this does not remain theoretical and the risk taken by
God is not a "calculated risk," it implies that it really belongs
to humanity to bring to fulfillment God's creation, God's love,

God's self-sacrifice. At least one man must accept his "response-ability" in the partnership for the relationship desired and initiated by God not to be sterilized. It is how "Israel" starts to be: someone in the universe responds. Someone, by affirming God's creation, by proclaiming a creation that is not so much historical as it is existential, participates in that creation, and hence both affirms and proclaims God's reality. Far from merely describing a unique series of historical events, the one who proclaims God's action *be-r'ešit* ("in the beginning"), is co-creating with God. Like Adam's naming the animals and thereby giving them their reality through a cooperative act with God, the author of Genesis 1:1 *names* the creative action of God, and thus fully participates in that action.

Now, the "somebody" author of Genesis 1:1 is not as anonymous as he may seem to be. Textual criticism has revealed that he is a collectivity, in fact, a band of Israelite priests, responsible for a "codex" designated as "P." As a response to Israel's despair during the Babylonian exile in the sixth century B.C.E., these priests wrote an extensive narrative now present in the Scripture. Their hope was that the people might regain confidence, for if God is capable of creating the universe as a whole from nothing, he is powerful enough to revive the people.[3] The creating God is capable of raising the dead body of the exiles to a glorious life.

Such a critical look upon the "setting in life" of the text (see above, chapter 1) is necessary, for it provides the right perspective on how to read the myth of creation. Far from being a speculative intellectual reconstruction of the primordial events, this first chapter of Genesis becomes prospective; its emphasis is on Israel and its message is existential, historically oriented and liturgically structured. The acknowledgment of the existence of a world at large is no tribute paid with reluctance by a fundamentally particularistic people to a cosmos it could not afford to ignore, but represents for all practical purposes the surrounding world of Mesopotamia in which Israel had to live and find a meaning for her existence. In brief, Genesis 1 does not speak of creation in general, and the aim is not to satisfy our natural curiosity as to the origins of the universe. What is created is the world of the dialogue God-Israel. Gerhard von Rad is right when pointing out that before creation comes redemption.[4]

Such a critical statement is important in many respects. Suffice it to say for our purpose here that it at least confirms what can be learned from the study of many other texts: *history* brought Israel to state her confessions of faith. These have never been produced by philosophers of any kind, sitting in ivory towers. Genesis 1:1 is an existential response to an existential situation.

This becomes all the more potent if we take into consideration the dynamism of the Hebrew preposition *be* which opens the narrative on creation. *Be-r'ešit* says more than "in the beginning"; the expression speaks of a finality in the act of creation: "in view of (for) a beginning." Seeking a beginning to himself as Creator and Savior, God finds also and *consequently* a beginning to all things (*"ta panta"* of Col. 1:16ff.). Through his creative act, God wills the beginning of a history. Furthermore, this "beginning" is not simply the starting point of something: *r'ešit* contains its end, it is a recapitulation of all the history that is to come. At the moment when God creates a "beginning," he brings about a *telos,* a finished and perfect reality.

In fact, a study of all the occurrences of the word *r'ešit* in Scriptures makes clear that the English translation, "beginning," is insufficient and approximate. In Biblical usage, the word designates primarily the first fruits of the harvest. As a second meaning it also designates the firstborn of a family or of a nation, or again the preeminence of a people as compared with others (so Amalek, Elam, Egypt, Ammon: Gen. 49:3; Num. 24:20; Jer. 49:35; Pss. 78:51; 105:36; Dan. 11:41). In the book of Proverbs, the *r'ešit* is Wisdom (8:22); and as a response to it, the human *r'ešit* is "fear of the Lord."

The outcome of the process is to be found in the prophetic texts where we have the proclamation that the *r'ešit* is Israel herself (Jer. 2:3; Amos 6:1; Hos. 9:10).

In all these texts *r'ešit* embodies the condensed strength of the harvest, of the cattle, of the nations, of humanity as a whole. The best translation in English is probably "the prime" (as in the expression "to be in its prime"). It is Wisdom, say the Sages; it is Israel, say the prophets; it is Torah, say both. In the New Testament, the term, as might be expected, is applied to the Christ, as he is for its authors the embodiment of Israel on the one hand, and of the Torah on the other (Col. 1:15; 1 Cor. 15:20; Rev. 3:14).[5] Therefore, a more incisive translation of Genesis 1:1 would be: "With a view to the Prime, God created heavens and earth." This "prime," then, this fullness or perfection at which God aims in the process of creation, is none other than that man whom he seeks and finds in his people. To put this another way, what Israel says in this opening chapter of her Scriptures is this: I want to be the beginning of the reality of God and of my reality. I want to give effectiveness to the becoming of God by my becoming. I want God to find his beginning in me. Yea, in view of me, God created! Through me, he wants to be.

From the very "beginning," God charges his creatures to bring his creating and redeeming actions to their fulfillment, to promote his love to its acme, to realize God's *r'ešit.* Only by so doing may humanity become its true self.[6] It is in this perspective that Israel considers her history: her becoming is humanity's "birthing." No one, said those who constituted the *"verus Israel,"* no one can be a person except by sharing in the struggle to become a person-with-God. That is what chosenness is all about; like creation, it is bi-dimensional; the chosen choose to be what they are.

When Israel, meeting her destiny, chooses wandering in the wilderness over against residing in the lush civilization of Egypt, she fulfills collectively the vocation of all humanity. She chooses freedom rather than slavery; to co-create with God out of the formless and the void rather than to fabricate tombs for the dead. She prefers *praxis* to *stasis,* sanity to insanity, hope to despair, creation to conservation, history to magic, soul to machine, life to death, human being to no-being.[7] Such a choice is fully and finally *human,* because only such a choice humanizes life. Israel (or the choice embodied in that human reality)

is the Human Being every individual person is *in posse.* Every
one of us is confronted by the ethical duality (*not* "dualism") of
Deuteronomy 30: good and evil, life and death—everyone must
choose. Gathered before God, people of all space and time are
solicited by God, and all answer something; even silence is an
answer. From one end of history to the other, God is the Great
Beggar. For this, all of us have been called to freedom (see
chapter 4, below) so as to be able to respond positively or nega-
tively to God and to his creation. It is actually here that the
whole weave and the whole gamble of our history is found:
either to lead creation entrusted to us to its initial and final
perfection, or else to annihilate all things and kill God. For God
is love, he dies if love is not realized in his human counterpart.

The question, therefore, is to know who are the ones who
proclaim God Creator. Who says "yes" to God? By what name
do we acknowledge the concrete manifestation of this positive
commitment? Or again: who is the Prime the Creator is looking
for in making the immensity of heavens and earth? *Israel* is the
name of the human commitment to God. Alone in the mass of
those who say "no" or who go no further than to say "yes, but
. . . ," Abraham makes of his "yes" an unconditional response
by leaving all that binds him to negation.[8] This is precisely
where the adventure called "Israel" begins. Abraham's response is fruitful and creative. Abraham's commitment has a
future, "that he might see his seed, prolong his days, and that
the purpose of the Lord might prosper by his hand." (Isa. 53:10,
my translation) His descendants are not a race or a nation bound
merely by kinship. They are a posterity of loyalty, a brotherhood of faith. In this nation of believers, men and women are
continually being integrated who have not come out of the loins
of Abraham. Some of them are well known, like Melchizedek
the Jebusite, Tamar the Canaanite, Jethro the Midianite, Rahab
the Amorite, Ruth the Moabite; others are anonymous because
they are too numerous to mention—the multitudes of Egyptian
slaves who cast their lot with Israel and were thereby assimilated,[9] the Gibeonites (Josh. 9), the Canaanites who were
integrated at the conquest under Joshua, the *"gerim"* (aliens)

for whose welfare the Torah is so concerned,[10] the foreign wives whom one finds from one end of the history of Israel to the other, and many others (to speak only of the Biblical times). Israel therefore is not a race, but a function, a style of life, a "doing," a choice, an experience. *It is in this sense that I continually use the term "Israel" in this book.*

She is nonetheless a historical, concrete reality, not a disincarnated ideal. Her choice is an act which reflects upon her. All dichotomy is here overcome: the action (history) is the person (ontology). Humanity's existential option (its *"projet"* says Sartre) is operative, effective. The Bible is the record of such a historical option. Israel reflects upon Israel. True, not every member of that people (ancient or modern) has the stature of an Isaiah. There is only one Moses in all of history. But the great Isaiah and the giant Moses are nothing without their "stiff-necked" people: " 'If you will not forgive their sin, I pray you, blot me off your book.' " (Exod. 32:32) The Scriptures do not describe a soul-saving process of aristocratic individuals concerned with their hereafter, but present us instead with a community engaged in the here and now of history, and led, willy-nilly, to encountering their destiny by prophets, priests, kings, and others still, who were at once hated and loved, cursed and revered, rejected and followed.

It certainly helps to be reminded by Morton Smith that there were parties and factions in ancient Israel just as there are today.[11] It is useful to remember in this context that Israel then as now needed prophets and sacrifices and repentance and admonitions and God's wrath; but to draw from this the conclusion that "Israel" is a myth, an "ideal" carefully constructed by a few postexilic priests and thereafter entertained by utopians living no earlier than the third century B.C.E., is an unwarranted stretching of the evidence. Moses and Isaiah, David and Jeremiah, Samuel and Amos are not creations of the postexilic community in Jerusalem.

Moreover, at no time in her history has Israel pretended to be superhuman. Never was the human role confused with that of angels. To become fully human has always been acknowledged by Israel as being beyond mere human achievement: "Prepare yourself and stand up like a man" says God to Job (Job 40:7*a*, my translation). It is self-evident that people in general, and every individual, even the "best," in particular, at times preferred to "serve other gods" and to deal with more predictable and fathomable deities. But, if our reading of the Bible needs the demythologization of the sort I am performing here, this must not open doors to a mythology in reverse. I mean that even though Israel has never been a group of charismatic saints and has always needed prophets, priests, sages, and kings, still, it would be false to think that, with a few exceptions, the people were a band of ignoramuses. The very language used by their leaders, wise men, and prophets in addressing them does not allow for such a reductionistic view of Israel.

In other words, at the time of the Scriptures, as much as in today's Jewish or Christian communities, faith and commitment are never shared by the majority. Such a stand is never and nowhere popular. But it has the amazing power to stir the imagination of masses and to make them eager to participate in the venture, even if with extreme weakness, stiffneckedness and "limpingness" (cf. 1 Kings 18:21). They both participate in and disengage themselves from the enterprise. But be that as it may, they *are* the people admonished by the prophet, the object of God's love and wrath, the carriers of the Name ("Semites").

Because of this ambiguity, the Levites are *gerim* (strangers) in the midst of their own people (cf. Judg. 17:7–9; 19:1).[12] Their deprivation of all property, their poverty and dependency, their status of being constantly in need of the grace of God and the generosity of others, made them aliens among their own people. Beyond and over their cultic functions, they represented an essential dimension of Israel. For Abraham had been a *ger* in Hebron (Gen. 23:4); Moses in Midian (Exod. 2:22; 18:3); the Israelites in Egypt (Exod. 22:21; 23:9; Deut. 10:19; 23:7). Without proprietors, there is still Israel (Israel in the wilderness, Israel of the exile and the diaspora), but without Abraham, Moses, and the Levites, without the deprivation, there is no Israel.

On this plane again, the message of Israel to " 'all the families of the earth' " (Gen. 12:3) is totally human. It is not esoteric; it speaks of no initiation into mysteries; it proclaims no philosophical wisdom accessible only to an intellectual elite; it asserts no aristocratic ideal valid only for the well-to-do few. The doctrine of Israel " 'is not too hard for you, neither is it far off. It is not in heaven. . . . Neither is it beyond the sea. . . . But the word is very near you; it is in your mouth and in your heart, so that you can do it.' " (Deut. 30:11–14)

What was at stake with the appearance of Israel in the world was not the addition of a new people to the chronicle of nations. Something new had been born. A new element had entered the cosmos, the demonstration that humanity is not under the determination of *stasis,* of insanity, despair, magic, machine, and death. With the appearance in the world of Israel, human beings are no longer under the determination of meaninglessness. In a very radical way a new creation starts with God's first words to Abram in Genesis 12:1 after the chaotic turmoil of the preceding chapters. A new humanity is born which lives side by side with the constructors of Babel. It is formed by all those who, with "the father of faith," become the Prime in view of which God created, the leaven of the universal dough, the community of the righteous saving the world. All creation rests on their shoulders, for their answer is given in the name of all people. Creation owes to them its continuance, since without them the world would immediately return to chaos (Gen. 12:2; 6:7–8; 18, etc.). Thanks to them, on the contrary, the whole world advances towards its *telos.*[13] "As for me," says God to Noah, "behold, I establish my covenant with you. . . . neither shall all flesh be cut off any more by the waters of the flood." (Gen. 9:9, 11, my translation)

God's choosing is on a cosmic scale. And though Abraham alone fertilizes and is responsive to the choosing and consequently becomes the chosen of the Lord, it would be impossible to reduce the love of God to a gratuitous preferential choice excluding all the others. All people are "wicked" and it is one wicked man among others who accepts the great adventure of faith. The miracle of history is precisely that there is a righteous

one, then a family, a group, a nation who sustain the reality of
God and of all creation. Called Israel, she is never cut off from
the rest of the nations. She is not a special race, but the inclusive
family of those who proclaim that God created heavens and
earth for the sake of finding himself in his human creatures.
Hence the existence of these witnesses is made meaningful;
their choice demonstrates that they understand and assume
creation and their role in it. They know by the same token the
raison d'être of heaven and earth. They acknowledge their ties
with the whole of the universe, the latter being not only the
framework within which the God-human dialogue occurs, but
the cosmic extension of humanity. This is why a man is already
present the very first day of creation. He is the soul of the whole
body, the one for whom light is created, and stars and plants and
animals. All of these have meaning only if the man recognizes
in them an invitation to come fully alive through him.

In Israel's conception, *man* "is the image of the invisible
God, the first-born of all creation; for in him all things were
created, in heaven and on earth, visible and invisible, whether
thrones or dominions or principalities or authorities—all things
were created through him and for him." (Col. 1:15–16) In these
words Paul spoke of the Nazarene, the man *par excellence,* the
"Central Jew." But Paul simply applied to "Christ" predicates
which by nature, according to the Hebrew consciousness, belong to Israel and are properly applicable to her alone.

Israel is therefore a community in which all others have a
place, their proper place. However, universalism must pass
through particularism if it is not to be annihilated. What is asked
of historical Israel by God is that she firmly, jealously, exclusively, refer herself to her image as reflected in her Lover's eyes
(that is to say, to the Torah). The more the chosen one carries
out the separation implied by holiness, the better she accom-
plishes her missionary vocation! For her duty is priestly.

Alone among the nations of history, Israel stresses that
human existence is not to be equated with the gathering of
power, but with the dynamic free choice of becoming. Alone in
the concert of peoples, she has diverted humanity from the

illusion of protecting its status quo and its uncommitment through riches of all kinds. In Israel, people are not to be judged according to their property, their qualities or virtues, the amplitude of their knowledge, the power of their intelligence, but according to their will to become fully what they are. All possessions are looked upon with suspicion in Israel because they mark too well the refusal of the human adventure. Abraham is praised, not because of his moral virtues (cf. Gen. 21), but because of his voluntary deprivation (cf. Gen. 22). Moses is the archetypal leader, not because he has a powerful personality (cf. Exod. 11:3; Num. 20), but because he is humble (Num. 12:3) and a man of God (1 Chron. 23:14). To be sure, moral standards, human virtues, and material possessions also find their place in the historical process. But they are means to reach the goal, never an end in themselves. They are secondary and subservient (cf. Matt. 6:33). They make Israel "rich" and therefore add to her responsibilities in the covenant. She is now expected to provide peace round about her, to give *shalom* to all those who are handicapped—materially or morally, psychically or spiritually—in their dialogue with God.[14]

It is thus clear that Israel's chosenness, her being set aside as a "holy" nation of priests, in no way entails a metaphysical or cosmic dualism. Israel never thinks in those terms. The choice which she proposes to all people is not a selection, an eclecticism of any sort. The flesh is not disdained for the sake of the soul. Nature is not sacrificed on the altar of history. Rather, human beings are viewed as engaged in a historical process of spiritualization of the universe and of themselves. They are called to "become holy as God is holy." (Lev. 11:44; 19:2; 20:7, my translation; cf. 1 Pet. 1:16) Human destiny is to "share in the very being of God" (cf. 2 Pet. 1:4; 2 Cor. 3:18; John 1:12, 13). This point will be developed in the following chapter.

3. The Kingdom of Priests

"You shall be to me a kingdom of priests."
[Exod. 19:6]

The text of Exodus 19:4–6 is the majestic portico opening on a great theophany. In fact, we have here the liturgy of an old festival celebrating the renewal of the covenant between God and Israel. Exodus 19 constitutes the introit, after which come the solemn proclamation of the Torah (chapter 20), the commitment of the people (chapter 24), the making of the covenant *(ibid.),* in all likelihood followed originally by benedictions and curses.

The meaning of our text depends largely upon its *Sitz im Leben* and its date of composition. The association of the words "kingdom" and "priests" has a markedly different effect in the time of the postexilic high priesthood from the one it had under the united monarchy.

Scholars have recognized in Exodus 19 the *Bundesformular* (covenantal formulary) of the treaties as they stemmed from the Hittites' pacts with their vassals and spread through Assyria, Syria, and Israel.[1] As far as Exodus 19 is concerned, there are traces of a Shechemite cultic tradition. Thus, for Gerhard von Rad for example, the expression "a holy nation" has such an origin.[2] And for Martin Noth as well, these words are the counterpart of another formula in use in Shechem: "people of God."[3]

Whatever its ultimate derivation, it is clear that Exodus 19: 4–6 is an important cultic, and probably recurrent, proclamation. Its style raises difficult problems, and Hans Wildberger comes to the conclusion that we have here a tradition *sui gen-*

eris, although with deuteronomic parallels.[4] (Cf. Deut. 10:14–
15; 28:9–10; 4:20; 26:19; 27:9; Josh. 24; 1 Kings 8:53.) Above all,
the comparison is striking with Deuteronomy 7:6 = 14:2 (my
translation): "For you are a holy people to the Lord your God:
the Lord your God has chosen you to be his private property,
out of all peoples that are upon the face of the earth."[5]

In favor of an early dating of Exodus 19:6 is the use of the
expression *mamlekheth kohanim* (kingdom of priests). The
conjunction of the two notions appears in texts such as Psalm
110; Jeremiah 33:17–22; Zechariah 4:14; and Chronicles (David
as the organizer of the Levitical functions in Israel). It is to be
noted that Psalm 110 has probably been written for David's
coronation.[6]

Indeed, I consider too precipitate the conclusion of some
critics that the expression "a kingdom of priests" reflects a situation after the exile in Babylon.[7] Israel would here be described
as "a nation where the priests are the actual kings." The relationship between kingship and priesthood has been a difficult
one since the creation of a king in Israel and, in the best of cases,
has existed as a dialectical tension.[8] Moreover, all records concur in pointing out that *Israel as a whole* is priestly (cf. Hos. 4:6)
and kingly (cf. Num. 24:7–9), as well as prophetic (Num. 11:29).
Israel herself disposes of the appointment of kings, " 'the shout
of a king is among them.' " (Num. 23:21) Thus kings and priests
in Israel considered themselves to be representative of their
people's inherent qualities.

These qualities are the fruit of the loving relationship between Israel and her God. Her intimacy with God is "priestly"
because as a rule only priests have that kind of relation with
Yhwh; and she is kingly because she constitutes the realm
where God's kingship is at work. Her priesthood and her kingship among the nations are thus the blessings of her dialogue
with God. Martin Buber is right (as against Hans Wildberger)
when he insists upon the stance towards the nations that such
titles imply.[9]

The immediate context of the expression *mamlekheth kohanim* in Exodus 19 has a decisive bearing here. The mention of

the universe doubtless puts the expression in the light of the relationship of Israel to the world. Such a connection is explicitly stated as the ultimate goal of God's sovereignty over Israel: " 'for all the earth is mine.' " (Exod. 19:5) The separation of Israel *from* the rest of the nations is never for its own sake. It is eventually a dedication *to*, a sanctification *for*, all the others.[10] Such is also the idea involved in the notion of the kingship of God as proclaimed in Israel's festivals (cf. Pss. 22:29ff.; 103:19ff.; 47:3ff.; 93; 96; 97; 98; 99). Israel is the locus of the universal kingship of God; I shall come back to this below.[11]

It would surely be incorrect to shrink the meaning of the word *kohen* (priest) in Exodus 19:6. But Martin Buber in his *Moses* proposed to understand the term, on the basis of 2 Samuel 20:26 in contrast with 1 Chronicles 18:17; 27:33, as designating "the foremost ones at the king's hand," i. e., the ministers.[12] Such a broadening of meaning is possible, but it must be clearly noted that the term "priest" is used in these passages (as in 2 Sam. 8:18; 20:26) with a tint of its own and for specific reasons. In any case, the word keeps its fundamental sense of "priest," and points to the idea of representativity, of honor, of mediation conveyed by the term *kohen*.

As a matter of fact, Exodus 19:6 is not speaking merely of a "kingdom of sacrificers," for example. Such an interpretation would confuse the priestly function as such with one of the characteristics of that function—sacrifice. In fact, the priest, according to the Scriptures, is not merely an official attached to the altar. Edmond Jacob states that the priest in Israel, even the first of them, Moses (whose priesthood passed to Aaron), "communicates God's oracles (Ex. 33.7), he sprinkles the blood of sacrifice (Ex. 24.6), he intercedes for the guilty people with the object of obtaining its pardon (Ex. 32.20)." Thus, the priest is "a man of a function" which is characterized by "teaching and intercession." Even the priest's apparel indicates the eminence of his position: "the breastplate with the names of the twelve tribes means that he assumes the responsibility of the people as a whole; the diadem comparable to the headdress of the Nazirites symbolizes the integrity of the vital force."[13]

Edmond Jacob's outline allows us to complete the sketch. The priest is "freed" of all sociological contingencies; he has no part in the territorial inheritance of Israel although he is an integral member of the people.[14] *In* the world, he is already no longer *of* the world. His position is extremely precarious. Should the nation wander from the covenant, the priest would immediately become utterly superfluous and parasitical (he is potentially "alien" in any case). Consequently, he will be feared because of what he represents, and hated because of his difference. Besides, it is only the people's failure that justifies his functions. He reminds them constantly of their weakness and their guilt. At a deeper level, one could say that, like monarchy (cf. 1 Sam. 8; 10:17–27; 12), priesthood is born in Israel of the wrath of Yhwh against the faithlessness and the revolt of his creatures; it must thus be seen dialectically as at the same time conveying a blessing and recalling a calamity (cf. Exod. 4:14). God is the only "Priest," his priesthood does not have the negative aspect present in human ministry. He is the master of Torah, the teacher of his people, the forgiver of their sins (cf. Exod. 32:14; 2 Sam. 24:16; Jer. 15:6; John 3:17). Israel as a whole is the reflection (the image) of the divine priesthood (cf. Exod. 19:6; Num. 3:11ff.). The Israelite cultic officers, therefore, by stepping as it were between God and Israel, make the bearing of God's and Israel's priesthood *indirect* instead of direct. Similarly, the kings make God's and Israel's kingship an indirect sovereignty.

But the presence of the priests is not merely a sign of unfulfillment, it is also the promise and the foretaste of the accomplishment. These commissioned ministers constitute in themselves the assurance of the actual presence in Israel of the priestly kingdom. For as no king is king except in relationship to the true King, so no one is priest unless he is the representative of the true Priest.

If so, what is the use of priesthood in Israel? What is its meaning and its *raison d'être?* We just saw that Edmond Jacob distinguishes three major functions of the priest: sacrificing, teaching, interceding. To understand this threefold activity, we must trace it back to its historical origin—the exodus. The exodus is the central event of Israel's history.[15] It constitutes the main point of reference in the creeds (cf. Exod. 20:2ff.; Num. 23:22; 24:8; Deut. 26:5ff.; 6:21ff.; Josh. 24; Judg. 6:13; 1 Sam. 4:8; 2 Sam. 7:23; cf. 2 Sam. 7:6, etc.) which make it the axis of history. All the constitutive elements of Israel as a people dedicated to God are born here. All of them have the status of an achieved prototype. The institutions are already wholly present: the king-priest-prophet in the person of Moses;[16] the Levite-substitute in the person of Aaron (Exod. 4:14) and the Levitism (Exod. 32—33); the priesthood (Exod. 28—29; 39); the elders keeping the common law (Exod. 3:16); the Torah (Exod. 19—24; 34); the Temple (Exod. 25—27; 30—31; 35—38; 39—40); the festivals (Exod. 12—13; 31); the sacrifices (Exod. 18; 27; 29). It is all the more striking to discover that all these institutions, which express the very soul of Israel, are, in an appropriate way, related to priesthood, that is, primarily to *substitution.* I have argued elsewhere[17] that the main theme of Exodus 1—15 is in fact the idea of substitution.[18]

Israel's way of being priest is to substitute for the world. Symbolically, Exodus 1—15 postulates that the very presence of Israel in Egypt constitutes the guarantee for the Egyptians' survival, but as soon as the Hebrews sever their ties with Egypt, Egypt dies in the persons of her firstborn children. For, as pointed out above, the firstborn carry within themselves all the potentialities of the nation (cf. Exod. 12:33). Israel—in her ancestor Joseph—is the shield protecting the integrity of Egypt. When the shield of priesthood is removed, God appears as the Terrible into whose hands it is awful to fall (Heb. 10:31; cf. Exod. 34:10; Ps. 76:8; Dan. 9:4, etc.).

This does not mean, however, that Israel does not herself need to be protected by priesthood. Israel needs a substitute in order that she may not die by seeing God face to face (cf. Exod. 33:20). The priestly people must have in its midst a priesthood-substitute, and that's exactly the function of Levitism (cf. Num.

3:12, 41, 45; 8:16–17; 16:48). Aaron's role is to replace all the Israelite firstborn, and above all the *"bekhor" par excellence*, the representative of Israel: Moses, whose birth after Aaron's and Miriam's is presented, however, as the birth of a firstborn (see Exod. 2:1 in Hebrew).[19]

Aaron, in fact, is in the center of a larger circle constituted by the descendants of Levi. They in turn are the substitutes for the people; they embody the *r'ešit* of the nation, of which they are the finest point, the most accurate expression. Even in the desert after the emergence from Egypt, they lead Israel in an endless and uncompromising wandering towards a goal eternally beyond reach: the promised land (cf. Exod. 32:26ff.). The Levitical priesthood constitutes the "thirteenth" tribe around which the twelve are gathered (cf., e.g., Josh. 14:1–3), the Levites themselves circling around their "father," Aaron, himself a substitute for Moses, and the latter being "covered by God's hand until he has passed by." (Exod. 33:22, my translation) By concentric circles we thus narrow in from Egypt (=the nations) to Israel as the People, from the latter to the Levites in their midst, to Aaron, to Moses, and eventually to God, the sole Priest. But this geometric description is somewhat misleading, for in point of fact it is the inner circles which protect the outer ones and not conversely. The world is in the center of God's concern. The priest has been appointed to the parish, rather than the parish to the priest. The Levites are an offering for the sake of Israel (Num. 8:10–11), and like Moses they do not supersede the People in the relationship with God (cf. Exod. 32:10–15). They foreshadow Israel's dynamic move towards accomplishment, when the whole nation will be priest for Yhwh, and its priesthood extended to all the earth (cf. Isa. 61:6).[20] Priesthood, like all other ministries characteristic of Israel, is exerted in a process, in a tension towards its fulfillment. Priesthood is eschatological, that is, an actual reality experienced as historical *and* thrusting towards its self-transcendence.

This means that priesthood is both exclusive and universal. Priesthood therefore represents a gift and a promise, a *Gabe* which is *Aufgabe*, an exclusive character of the people-priest but also a power destined to fill the whole world. To the universality of Israel's priesthood I shall return in a moment. About its exclusiveness, however, it must be noted that Torah, which ought to be written in everyone's heart, remains until the coming of the messianic age a body of instruction which needs to be taught by appointed priests to a people who have been called precisely to know without being taught! The paradox therefore is that "professional" ministers must in a way whet the appetite of the people for their own heritage. But one day this Torah will be "put ... in their inward parts, and ... [written] in their hearts" (Jer. 31:33, KJV) so that " 'no longer shall each man teach his neighbor and each his brother, saying, "Know the LORD," for they shall all know me [God], from the least of them to the greatest.' " (Jer. 31:34) For the Torah is not imposed upon people from "outside," as a super-nature superseding human nature and tearing people between their finitude and an impossible infinite. On the contrary, far from being an "ideal," Torah is the unveiling of what is truly and by creation, by vocation and by grace, Israel, that is, *humanity* in its fullness.

From this vantage, it is clear that priesthood is universal. No wonder therefore if the eschatological dimension of it is the restoration of its universality as we have seen it expressed by Jeremiah.[21] In the meantime, the nations and the twelve tribes are standing around the central tribe of Levi and find in the latter the reflection of their true image. Together around the priests, all receive a teaching, which is not the teaching of a gnosis, foreign to us and dispensed by masters of thought, nor an escape from the hard realities of daily life. The priestly existence is entirely put under the sign of *abodah,* which in Hebrew means labor as well as worship. The priest teaches how to work, how to act, how to live, and this is worship. Faithful to her non-dualistic conception of existence, Israel makes no distinction between activity and cult. The authentic action of humanity is worship of God; conversely, nothing in human existence is "profane"; hence the all-inclusive laws of the Torah leave no "department" of life outside the sphere of God's demands for sanctification.[22]

Even the priests, to be sure, do not comply with such a total commitment to God. They also, like their particular or universal "parish," need atonement for their shortcomings (cf. Lev. 4:3ff., 26; 5:6, 13, 16; 6:7). The priests must first purify themselves (cf. Num. 8:6; 1 Chron. 15:14), then they in turn sanctify the people (cf. Exod. 19:10–15). On any occasion, they precede the people of whom they constitute the spearhead (cf. Josh. 3). In all things, therefore, the priests are the first ones engaged and exposed. They really are the *avant-garde* of the nation.

Due to his position between God and the people (like the ark of the covenant which he carries), the priest is quite naturally in charge of teaching and interceding. Being the first to receive the Word which he will then transmit, he is also the first object both of the heavenly blessings and cursings, presenting in his person, as an offering to God, all the weakness of creation. At this point, we come to the central character of priesthood. The priest's exposure to the infinite danger of the sacred[23] enables him to manifest for the people the frightening proximity of God (cf. Exod. 34:29ff.). It belongs to the ambiguity of the priest that he is loved for bringing God near, and feared because the nearer God is the more clearly it is realized that he remains the wholly "other" (cf. Isa. 6; 8:13; 29:23; Ps. 99). Such a staggering discovery explains the different functions of the priest. He sacrifices because " 'man shall not see me [God] and live.' " (Exod. 33:20) He teaches the people the oracles of God *(toroth)* applicable to any circumstance of existence because the whole of humanity is, through the mediation of the priest, put in communication with the holy. He intercedes for the people because, despite their allegiance to God, they are unfaithful to him (cf. Exod. 33:11–14).

Of the threefold ministry of the priest, the communication of God's oracles is the most important function, as Jeremiah 18:18 shows (my translation): "for instruction *(torah)* shall not perish from the priest, nor counsel from the wise, nor the word from the prophet." The priest instructs the people for its sanctification (cf. Lev. 13:16, 20). He takes Moses' place and fulfills his leadership in all collective and private spheres (cf. Lev.

10:8–11; Deut. 31:9, 25, 26). His vocational purpose is to show the real value of everything in God's eyes. And, since God judges everything in history, the teaching of the priest concerns itself with the totality of human experience. The God in whose name he speaks is a "jealous God," that is, an all-demanding God.

We thus come to a preliminary conclusion on Israel's priesthood in the world. Election is for a task, specifically a sacerdotal one. In the midst of all nations, Israel offers to God the totality of creation as a "reasonable sacrifice," i. e., dedicates to the Creator a world which tends to think of itself as closed and self-sufficient. Her function of intercessor is clearly another aspect of the same ministry. Israel prays for the world, like Abraham for Sodom and Gomorrah (Gen. 18). Indeed, she substitutes herself for the world, "shielding" as it were all the "Egypts" of space and time against the just wrath of the divine judge. She responds for and on behalf of the world to the eternal Lover, and thus performs a redemptive function in the universe. This latter, however, is not an illustrious event in a plot with two characters only, God and Israel. For the priestly function implies also and above all the teaching of God's will. The world's sanctification is not done by someone else and without its participation. As the love of God is not exclusive in terms of nations, it is also all-inclusive in terms of the total human experience. The whole of humanity in the whole of the world is solicited by Israel's God to respond to him. The chosen people thus strive for the time when "the earth shall be full of the knowledge of the LORD as the waters cover the sea." (Isa. 11:9)

In the meantime, only the people of Israel, only those who share in the *projet* of Abraham, are exposed to the "sacred." Only they, in this in-between time, "hear and hear, and *do* understand, see and see, and *do* perceive" (cf. Isa. 6:9). They share in the vision which consumes (cf. Exod. 3:2–6). For, as for now, the "sacred" is foiled by a "profane," i. e., by a deliberate rejection of God's expectations. "Sacred" and "profane" are not two realms opposed to each other, but as zones become darker and darker the more they are distant from the source of light, so there are concentric circles around the point of insertion of the sacred in the world. I shall come back to this point later.

The aim of the priestly function is clearly indicated: "Therefore, be holy as I am holy, says the Lord." (Lev. 11:44–45; 19:2; 20:26; 21:6, my translation) That is to say, be God's presence and action on earth. Be the *r'ešit* of creation, be the image of God.[24] Israel would forfeit any claim to be God's people in losing her priesthood. History has actually shown that Israel can live without kings or prophets, but she cannot live without priests. "When the monarchy no longer existed and when prophetic inspiration was beginning to weaken, the priest eclipses king and prophet and dons to some extent their mantles."[25] Every Jew is not necessarily a king or prophet, but *every Jew is a priest.* True, an expression like "people of Israel" does not seem to entail a conception of priesthood. It is therefore tempting to conclude that we have here a parallel notion which circulated in non-priestly milieux. Right up to the present, definitions of Jewish identity have followed these two lines conceived as independent from each other. Sometimes Jews are defined by their relationship with God; sometimes they are seen simply as members of a particular national or ethnic community. This is, however, a false dichotomy. According to Scripture, the people lose every national quality when there is no priesthood. "People" as used here always means God's people. The word does not refer to a characteristic shared by Israel with all nations of the world. At a time when the Hebrews were enslaved in the midst of the Egyptians, the term *'am,* people, was applied to the former to distinguish them from the latter (Exod. 1:9); this is because Israel's priestly dimension makes her something different from a *goy* in the midst of *goyim.*[26] When Israel is "complete," on the contrary, even the *goyim* around are the beneficiaries of her priesthood. The Egyptians did not know that the Hebrews' presence in their midst was actually saving the lives of their firstborn, the "prime" of Egypt. When it is too late, they realize that their pogrom has been a suicide.[27] Israel brings life to another region of the world and transforms Canaan into the Holy Land, lighthouse for eternity.

We thus understand why the priestly office is at the same time a process of purifying creation by sacrifice and intercession. It is—however audacious a statement this seems—a "deification" of creation, since only what is holy can be in dialogue with the Holy, only what is deified can find itself on the level of God and receive the Word of life of God (cf. 2 Pet. 1:4; 1 Pet. 1:13; Acts 17:29; 2 Cor. 3:18). If so, it is clear that the priestly office is the new possibility bestowed by God for humanity to reestablish, in its own life and in the whole world, the primordial and genuine purity of the creation. The priest is the indispensable condition for sanctification. He is the mediator between the Liberator and his people, between the Husband and his wife. He is the man taken by God, possessed by God; the personal possession of the Lord in whom God recognizes his own image. This one man who gives to all the measure of their stature in creation is at the benefit of the grace which transcends all contingencies: Moses' murder of the Egyptian *becomes* the accomplishment of the divine design (Exod. 2:12); the sword of Ehud is the word of God to Eglon (Judg. 3:20–21). Priesthood is not subsumed under ethics, but priesthood engenders its own ethics. The question is not to comply with a set of moral rules in order to be or to remain a priest. The question is to be faithful to the priestly covenant and to act accordingly, that is, to invent a response (a *torah*) to each soliciting problem of history and existence. Such an invention is a creative act under the inspiration which stems naturally from intercourse with God.[28]

Thus Israel has become the chosen people and it is no longer in her power to refuse the choice. Israel can no longer get rid of what is clinging to her flesh. The creating Word has made the Priest—Israel—and they are now one and the same reality: Israel in herself no longer exists; the priest in himself no longer exists. The two terms are inseparable. *It is Israel which depends on the vocation which she has received for eternity; the vocation does not depend upon the faithfulness of Israel.* Gomer is and remains, despite all the circumstances, the wife of Hosea. The covenant does not fall into abeyance as long as the Husband is ready to forgive his unfaithful spouse. Her harlotry places her in the juridic situation of being *Lo-'ammi* (not my people) and *Lo-ruhama* (not pitied); but where sin is multiplied grace immeasurably exceeds it. *Lo-'ammi* in Hosea 1:9 becomes *'Ammi* in Hosea 3:3; *Lo-ruhama* becomes *Ruhama.* God opens abscesses, he cuts into living flesh, and the wounds which he inflicts are terrible. When he rages, "the whole head is sick, and the whole heart faint. From the sole of the foot even to the head, there is no soundness in it, but bruises and sores and bleeding wounds; they are not pressed out, or bound up, or softened with oil." (Isa. 1:5–6) But nothing that he does to his people is irreparable: "the LORD binds up the hurt of his people, and heals the wounds inflicted by his blow." (Isa. 30:26; cf. Jer. 30:12, 16, 17) The Lord never cuts the umbilical cord which links Israel to the source of life.

Yhwh and Israel are as a matter of fact two who have become one. Israel is Yhwh in action. God is Life and Israel the existent; God is Love and Israel the beloved; God is Truth and Israel the authentic; God is Holiness and Israel is holy. The irreversibility of the covenant therefore is not a matter of feelings either in God or in Israel. God and Israel belong to each other as the cause and its effect. To be sure, faithfulness is not automatic, but neither is life automatic. There are alternatives of plus-being and minus-being in Israel's history as much as in our existence. It happens that the holy body becomes sick (Isa. 1:5–6), but God raises up a remnant, thus transfusing a new blood into Israel. At the limit, even if there is only one person, the Messiah in "a generation wholly wicked" *(be-dor kulo rasha')* as the Talmud puts it, there is nevertheless someone who remains the vis-à-vis of God and who makes God victor in the battling quest for himself in his creatures.

Neither the remnant nor the Messiah can be considered in themselves. They are no more sufficient in themselves than the umbilical cord attached to the embryo. The priest is nothing, the remnant is nothing, the Messiah is nothing . . . if they are not salvation for the whole of the people, if they do not validly represent the priesthood of the whole people. The remnant is not necessarily the "best" of Israel. It is the incarnate reminder of the vocation of the whole of Israel.

There is always someone in Israel who is carrying the vocation of all; in every generation, there is a substitutive victim (cf. above), a righteous savior, there is a priest who *lives* his function, whose teaching is not a gnosis or a bulk of information to be assimilated, whose intercession is not mechanical. And this only makes God's wager on humanity successful (cf. Job 1:12; 2:6). For God has put his life at stake in creating a partner whose response alone is able to create God in return. The seriousness of God's love may be gauged by his willingness to submit to the affirmation or negation of the beloved, so that he becomes the Being, or is rejected back to his positive Nothingness—to use an expression of the Zohar. Thus, yes, everything indeed depends on the fulfillment of the priestly vocation of Israel. But the triumph of love is that nobody can remain indifferent to it. On an existential plane, it is impossible for love to return to the lover fruitless, without effect (cf. Isa. 55:10–11). Victory is inherent to love, for love is the opposite of sterility and meaninglessness. Always, ever, generation after generation, the community of Israel—or a remnant in its midst, or a group of *Lamed Vav,*[29] or one individual repeating the adventures of Abraham—becomes the respondent of God. Even when she is unfaithful—and there is no other judge of this but God—Israel is the assurance of the world's salvation.[30] She is, in her becoming, the process of the return to God and of the salvation of the world. It is only within the context of a world belonging to the Creator that the life of Israel has meaning. It is therefore not surprising that the divine affirmation of the universality of his love is placed right in the middle of the most "particularist" declaration there is: "ye [Israel] shall be a peculiar treasure unto me above all people." (Exod. 19:5, KJV) The election is inclusive; all peoples are concerned. Ever since the beginning, Abraham was

chosen so that in him " 'all the families of the earth . . . [could]
bless themselves.' " (Gen. 12:3) The *ad extra* of the choosing of
Israel is expressed in the very words describing her becoming:
"ye shall be unto me a kingdom of priests, and a holy nation"
(Exod. 19:6, KJV)—Israel is the fulfillment of the vocation of the
created—*in order that all creation become Israel.* The chosen
people is the promise and the first fruit in the world of the
reparation of that which has been broken, the pole of attraction
for reconciled, disalienated people. This is not to say, however,
that Israel is mythical. Like any other nation under the sky she
is a living demonstration of failure. But here, and only here,
there is no hiatus between failure and victory. As Paul Ricoeur
writes: "With Isaiah, the salvation of a 'remnant' is *contemporary with* the destruction of the Temple, as the survival of the
stump is contemporary with the fall of the tree; while with the
Second Isaiah the new day is born *in* sorrow."[31] It is therefore
not a myth, for "myth puts in succession that which is contemporaneous and cannot not be contemporaneous." Instead, "in
the Instant I am created, in the Instant I fall. In the Instant I
am created: my pristine goodness is my status as a created
being; but I do not cease to be a created being unless I cease
to be; therefore I do not cease to be good. Then the 'event' of
sin terminates innocence in the Instant; it is, in the Instant, the
discontinuity, the breach between my having been created and
my becoming evil."[32] This statement of Paul Ricoeur's needs to
be completed by the restoration in the Instant brought about
by the covenantal relationship with God. *"Semper peccator,
semper justus,"* the Jew embodies or rather historicizes victory
in failure, not *after* failure. Jews do not jump from humanity
over to supra-humanity. They remain strictly on the human
level. Since their triumph is not the glorification of supra-
human achievements, no one feels excluded from their accomplishment. No one is led to feel like a "loser" over against
heroes. Jewish victory is not *over* failure, but *in* failure. Victorious Jews are helpless human beings. And this means also that
there are no human beings in the world who do not spiritually
become Jews!

Therefore, Israel, mirror of the true human identity, confronts all people with a gift, a challenge, and a judgment:

—Israel does not endure an existence involuntarily received and marked by death, but she lives by creating life. Others are thereby taxed to discover after her what it means really to live.

—She does not speak "the gibberish of human languages," as Georg Hamann said.[33] True, the Hebrew language is no mythical concept. It is not immune from the common linguistic woe. Hebrew, however, is the priestly human language. It is liturgical, the appropriate means for expressing a human existence conceived as wholly liturgical. As such, Hebrew *names* (i. e., it calls, or addresses a vocation to) all things. All human speech thus receives the revelation of that which it is trying so desperately to express.[34]

—She proclaims that God alone can say "I," while the empty human "I" must be filled by the abundance of the divine "I."

—She alone pronounces the Name that is "above every name that is named." (Eph. 1:21) Henceforth the names in all the pagan jargons are revealed in their true dimension as abortive attempts to pronounce the unpronounceable.[35]

—She sets aside one day, chosen among all those in the year, for the proclamation of the Tetragrammaton by the high priest in the Holy of Holies. Consequently, all the other days find their true image in this Yom Kippur, all other people in this sovereign sacrificer, and all other places in this center of the world.

For at one point in the *time* of the year, one *man* alone in humanity, representing one *nation* in the midst of the nations, goes forth towards a holy *place,* the navel of cosmic space, and pronounces the one *word* in the only *language* which is not a confused series of articulated sounds.

God is one—this is actually what is at stake with Israel's priesthood. In this People without elaborated creed, without systematic or constructive theology, this proclamation alone holds good: God is one. To be sure, this is no intellectual stance; the community must echo the oneness of God through its own oneness and the unification of the whole creation. The existence is one, the languages are one, the ultimate in humanity is one, the innermost toward which all efforts tend is one, the time is one, and the space is one. The oneness is the true identity of the creation now torn in pieces and dismembered through our own insanity. The salvation, that is, the restoration to the world of its true oneness, is performed by those who refuse in their own existence, in their own vital space, the atomizing of creation.

It is thus for all humanity that the high priest passes beyond the veil; it is to the yearly proclamation of the divine Name that creation owes its life. But Jewish thought recognizes that the day a non-Jew says: "In [view of] the beginning God created the heavens and the earth," that non-Jew becomes greater than the high priest, that day greater than Yom Kippur, and the place that witnesses the miracle holier than the Holy of Holies.[36] In this Gentile, Israel finds the purest fruit of her preaching (cf. Matt. 8:10; 15:28), for the priest's entire office is to confront all people with their priesthood, that is, as we have seen above, the choice to create with God.[37] In the person of the non-Jew sharing in the priesthood of Israel, history emerges into its accomplishment (cf. Isa. 66:18–21).

The chosen people are the concrete manifestation of the divine will not to impose love and law upon us, but to live them in the midst of all people, with all, within them. This "indwelling of God" (cf. Deut. 33:16)—the Zohar says *"tsimtsum,"* contraction, shrinkage—bears the name "Israel." Israel is the community of those who make manifest the presence of God in the supreme act of love, that is, death. God puts himself in failure in order that people, in their liberty, may triumph, and thus let God triumph—*God dies in order that people may live God!* God "contracts" himself in order to leave all the space to his partner in the relationship. Here is the staggering event which reveals what history is all about. The One whose essence is self-containment gives up his independence and his self-sufficiency for the sake of someone other, who by no means deserves such a sacrifice. But once the covenant has been established, the Masculine and the Feminine must encounter each other. It now becomes a necessity for the sake of his name, for his own sake (cf. Exod. 32:11–14). He is now so fully committed in his love for his undeserving partner, that he *is* love (1 John 4:8).[38]

The outcome of the communion of God with humanity is *r'ešit*, the Prime, or the *Tsemaḥ*, the Shoot, the King-Messiah who definitively makes true the prophecy. Meanwhile, the history of the steadfast love of God for his creatures, and of the equivocal response of humanity to God, is grounded on the total possibility for human beings to choose life or death, good or evil. Not a good or an evil, a life or a death, which would remain external to them, but *their* life and *their* death, that is, ultimately the life of God and death of God, for God has gone over to them! As for Israel, she chose to live (cf. Deut. 30:19), and to make God live.

Appendix to Chapter 3
Priestly Extraordinary
Acts in Scripture

The reports about the murders perpetrated by Moses, Ehud, Jael (Exod. 2:12; Judg. 3:12ff.; 4:17ff.) are so-called folk narratives. This means that, as examples of a popular literary genre, they share some characteristics common to the tales of all nations around the world. In the words of Robert H. Pfeiffer:

> the bulk of the narratives in the Old Testament (Gen.-I Sam.) is a rewriting of popular traditions and tales long transmitted orally. And this explains the obliteration of the line between reality and imagination in these stories. What holds a simple audience of Bedouins, shepherds, or peasants spellbound in listening to a tale is interest in the plot, curiosity as to the denouement, romantic atmosphere, conscious or unconscious art (as in the Andersen and Grimm fairy tales, respectively), but not in the least the historical accuracy. . . . Eventually outstanding literary men wove the folk tales, sagas, and legends into the great national epics recounting the heroic age of ancient Israel—the J and E documents in Genesis-Judges.[39]

This last development, however—in my opinion—completely changes the perspective. Tales which in their origins were "folk narratives" and meant "to please" a popular audience have been inserted into the "theological" reflection of Israel upon her identity. One cannot overlook the fact that Exodus 2 reporting Moses' murder of the Egyptian is now in the Pentateuch (Torah), that is, at the very core of Israel's description of her faith and order.

The nature of the report has changed in the process. Though perhaps a folk narrative in origin, Moses' "crime" (or Ehud's, or Jael's) becomes part and parcel of Israel's canon (standard, criterion) for faith and ethics. The former element is interesting, the latter is decisive. Ehud and Jael are both highly praised for their deeds (cf. Judg. 3:15, 28–29; 5:24ff.). In Exodus 2, Moses' act is presented in a very sober manner but no one can doubt that the author of the text has no reservations as to his hero's decision. Moreover—and this falls in line with my hermeneutical stand above—Israel's theological tradition (and for that matter the Church's) takes the murder of the Egyptian as a non-picturesque trait deserving to be theologically interpreted.[40]

André Neher writes:

> This wrath of Moses! Like all other signs of a passionate nature, it scares well-meaning people, who expect the "men of God" to be all honey and sweetness. But a little familiarity with the real nature of the Bible is enough to make one understand that these violent outbursts of wrath are the surest sign of a quest for the absolute.[41]

Thus, priestly acts which from an ethical point of view are most questionable or even condemnable (as in the examples given above) belong to another sphere of judgment, to another economy. Israel lives in no dualism, but she maintains that all human acts are ethically ambiguous. In the absolute, it is impossible to list in one column the "good" deeds and in the other the "evil" deeds. Good and evil are a matter of choice, not of nature. The best and the worst go side by side in every human act. The "ethical" nature of the deed depends finally upon the human dedication: is it to God, or to the self? Since Moses' or Ehud's murders are performed by their authors in a pure oblivion of themselves, they are priestly actions and they cannot derail the priestly accomplishment of Israel, let alone call into question the function itself. For in Hebrew Scriptures there is no dualism between the person and the person's function. Aaron becomes the mouth of Moses (Exod. 4:16), Moses becomes God for Pharaoh (Exod. 7:1), and Saul is changed into another man (1 Sam. 10:6, 9).

4. The Holy Nation

The previous chapter closed with the discovery that it is up to people themselves to choose life against death, to transform the world where they live from the chaos of no-life into the garden of Eden where they can thrive and make God live. Clearly, this raises the problem of liberty, and it is to this issue that I now turn, for it will, as we shall see, allow us to tackle the notion of holiness from a "right" perspective.

The Scriptures reveal a very distinctive conception of freedom, because they also know a view of death as not meaningless (cf. Deut. 30:18). They affirm that there is a death which is the culmination of life and which becomes, mysteriously, the spring of life, as when the seed rots in the earth and yields a well-filled ear. Such a "positive death" occurs each time a person goes through self-sacrifice for the love of God. This is for the Scriptures the supreme human act, and an act in which the human distinction from, and sovereignty over, the animal is convincingly demonstrated. For the animal can only undergo death; the animal's death is only an accident. Sartre's well-known exclamation, "All being is born without reason, prolongs its existence by weakness, and dies by accident," considers us solely as animals. (The same idea, interestingly enough, is expressed in similar terms in the Wisdom of Solomon 2:1–5 by the wicked!)

Not that human self-debasement to the rank of an animal is impossible. For, to be sure, it is part of our freedom that we can choose not to be free, but that is actually to die *"par recontre"* (by accident). People may consider themselves as mere pawns in a meaningless cosmology, trying desperately, before they are cut off "by chance," to prolong an existence that leads nowhere.[1] As early as the Genesis myth of creation, Israel made clear that irresponsibility, equated with animality, is *the* fatal temptation (cf. Gen. 3:1). It is the supreme temptation because it provides the complete surrender all are longing for from the moment they leave their mother's womb. It is no accident that those who claim to be "natural," the naturists à la Rousseau, claim to live in accord with cosmic rhythms and to attune their heartbeats to telluric pulsations. The mother-earth has become a surrogate uterus. The naturists have simply exchanged one womb for another. Here, all problems have an external cause. Human beings are not really responsible, they are enveloped securely in layers of natural laws, of scientifically explainable phenomena. "And the man said: 'The woman whom you gave to be with me, she gave me of the tree and I did eat.' . . . And the woman said: 'The serpent beguiled me, and I did eat.' " (Gen. 3:12, 13, my translation)

Now a certain discrepancy has been noted between God's warning to Adam and Eve "in the day that you eat thereof you shall surely die" (or "you shall immediately die"), and the delay granted to them after their actual disobedience. It is not wrong to see a gracious gesture of God in this delay but the latter has also and simultaneously another meaning: the very moment they started to disobey, death had already started to occur; death is as much behind them as still to come. In other words, the decease will be the verification of a past fact: through this wrong choice, they have already begun to die! The decease in this case is the stamp of nothingness affixed on an "absence."

So much for death as seen by a famous modern philosopher in its total negativity. But the Scriptures know of another, "positive," death. They know of the human uniqueness in the cosmos, a uniqueness attested to by the fact that of all creatures only people can take death upon themselves and transfigure it. Rather than bringing in Biblical allusions to such a transfiguration—one thinks, e. g., of the *locus classicus* Isaiah 52:13—53:12 —let me instead quote the "unbeliever" Albert Camus:

"What's natural is the microbe. All the rest—health, integrity, purity (if you like)—is a product of the human will, of a vigilance that must never falter. The good man, the man who infects hardly anyone, is the man who has the fewest lapses of attention. And it needs tremendous will-power, a never ending tension of the mind, to avoid such lapses. . . . All I maintain is that on this earth there are pestilences and there are victims, and it's up to us, so far as possible, not to join forces with the pestilences. . . . So I resolved always to speak—and to act—quite clearly, as this was the only way of setting myself on the right track. . . . That's why I decided to take, in every predicament, the victims' side, so as to reduce the damage done. . . . Can one be a saint without God?—that's the problem in fact, the only problem."[2]

Humanity alone is confronted with the miraculous possibility of changing the negative into the positive. Instead of helping chaos to triumph over creation by their amorphousness (cf. Gen. 1:2), human beings can actually co-create with God in giving life to what is dead, and primarily to themselves. In order to achieve this, they must renounce their murderous hatred of creation, of matter, of flesh, of themselves, of others; they must *love*, that is, they must discover the self-sacrificial meaningfulness of their existence, of their suffering and death. Sartre hates failure; the Jewish way of thinking fully embraces failure as being our life and our crown because it is God's life and crown! For the "nations," triumph is the opposite of failure; for the "Christianized" Gentiles, success is *beyond* failure.[3] But for Israel, for Jesus of Nazareth, for Rabbi Akiba, the victory is *in* the defeat. The prize is in the battle itself.[4] Job exclaims: "Though God slay me, I trust in him." (13:15, my translation) And André Neher records a Hasidic tale of a rabbi interceding for the sick child of a poor widow. "This child must die," answers heaven. But the rabbi persists until God tells him: "If you continue to pray, the child will be healed, but you will be irrevocably excluded from your part in the world to come." The rabbi prays, the child is healed, and the rabbi gathers his disciples for the mystical dance of Supreme Joy. Henceforth, assured that he is to die with his death, the rabbi will be able to serve God with an absolute disinterestedness.[5]

There is a dialectical polarity in failure. The death of the martyrs in Auschwitz and the death of Adolf Hitler in his bunker look like twins. The similarity goes so far as to be in both cases a death by fire. Hitler too had his crematorium. Nevertheless, and despite the similarities, the deaths are absolutely incomparable, one is meaningful and creative, the other a meaningless annihilation.

André Neher has brilliantly shown the positiveness of failure in the Bible and the Jewish perspective. Let me briefly summarize his thought. All of us have a natural repulsion for failure—the omnipresence of it sets ultimate limits on our aspirations and demonstrates the depth of our impotence. Our strategy is therefore always to disguise our failures, to adorn them with an appropriate makeup in order to forget them as soon as possible. Failure has no place in our philosophy of life and history. Life and history are, on the contrary, a continuous series of victories and successes. The Mesopotamian kings, the Egyptian Pharaohs paraded in clay and stone the record of their triumphs and achievements, but hardly ever said a word about their mistakes or defeats. In contrast to this, if Israel recounts her slavery in Egypt and in Babylon,[6] this is but a staggering exception in a general rule: nothing is more repulsive than to lose.

Christianity has revealed a deep nuance in this perspective. Christ proclaimed that to follow him one must be ready not only to hate one's relatives and loved ones, but even one's own life (Luke 14:26). The symbolism of the cross is used time and again to point to the death that must precede resurrection. One recalls Jesus' saying, " 'if they do this when the wood is green, what will happen when it is dry?' " (Luke 23:31) But to everyone's relief, the sting of death is removed: it is no longer final, no longer absolute; it is provisional, it is defeated by the afterdeath. Though all must die, it is only in order to be raised. Christians have become experts in "spiritualizing" death (and also sacrifice, suffering, poverty, renunciation). Defeat is transitory. " 'Blessed are those who mourn, for they *shall be* comforted.' " (Matt. 5:4, emphasis mine)[7] The mourning from this perspective has no value in itself, no more than poverty, meekness, or hunger for righteousness. They are only useful because they unlock, as it were, the mercy of God. "I consider that the sufferings of this present time are not worth comparing with the glory that is to be revealed to us." (Rom. 8:18)[8]

Compared with the negative stand vis-à-vis failure, this is a tremendous step forward. But is not death here still only a necessary evil, an inescapable condition for subsequent life? What remains ultimately important and praiseworthy for many a Christian is victory. The cross is but an accident, the sacrifice of one's self, the gate opening on paradise. The kingdom of God is beyond defeat. The Suffering Servant of Isaiah 53, it is stressed, will eventually "see his offspring, he shall prolong his days; [and] the will of the LORD shall prosper in his hand." (vs. 10) Even his innocence and his martyrdom are seen from an external point of view as guaranteeing his reward.

Again, uniquely among all the nations throughout history, Israel discovers and reveals victory *in* defeat, triumph *in* failure. Such a stand is possible because of her dramatic view of the relationship between people and God. In a dualistic conception of the divine and the world, failure plays no role, or only a transitory one; but in a "monistic" conception, failure does belong to and even permeates history. God himself, because he is one with his creation, is in failure or, at least, must cope with failure! Is this a contradiction in terms? It hardly seems that the magnificent fresco of Genesis 1—2 showing God creating the heavens and the earth will back up this conviction of ours about God. Seemingly, the perfect God is the author of a perfect creation: "And God saw that it was good. . . . God saw everything that he had made, and behold, it was very good." But quite soon the wonderful building erected by the great Architect reveals appalling flaws. The creation is so tenuous that its existence is endangered by the upsetting act of one among the creatures. Moreover, this one is not without accomplices, for the sin is echoed throughout the beautiful garden (cf. Gen. 3:12–13). Jewish tradition, reflecting on this primeval paradox, imagines that this creation by God has been preceded by twenty-six unsuccessful attempts. Now God expresses the wish, "may this one stand!" (*Gen. R.* 9:4) But, apparently, it does not stand any more than the preceding ones, for chaos (Gen. 1:2) remains threatening despite its defeat (cf. Ps. 104). Far from being restricted to prehistory, it is here and now the terrible possibility of failure, always present, always susceptible of being unleashed by Adam's hypocrisy (Gen. 3:8) and cowardliness (3:10), by Cain's violence, by the frightful indifference of Noah toward the dying world, by the general human uprising against God in building up its own conscience with a Tower of Babel, by the flabbiness of the generation of the wilderness.

According to the Biblical approach to reality, creation and life are a "perhaps," a sheer promise. But a promise is and must remain forever promise. It can never be resolved into its contrary, that is, into some "fullness"—for this would not only abrogate the promise from now on, but make it meaningless ever since it was given. The promise is never resolved into rest, into status quo. Thus, for example, the sabbath is not an absence of activity;[9] it is the bringing of work to completion, the movement of crowning action with sanctification. Inserting herself into this movement, Israel is ceaselessly pushed further toward another sabbath more whole than the preceding one. She thus goes from achievement to achievement in a way, as all sabbaths are achievements, but it is a dialectical kind of fulfillment which needs endlessly to open itself on a greater one, so that in fact accomplishment is at the same time failure or is contained in failure. It belongs to the dynamism of relationship to God that the goal can never be reached; choices must always be made anew and God must always be discovered and loved anew. "Woe to man who is not in quest, woe to man who does not find, woe to man who is complacent with what he found," says Denis de Rougemont.

Joshua and the people finally reach the promised land. The promise seems to be fulfilled and thus to vanish in nothingness. Yet all is not set for Israel: it is not yet the promised land but in a way all too conspicuously the land of the Canaanites, the

Hittites, the Jebusites. The promise has not disintegrated into the accomplishment. The Israelites have still to conquer, to sanctify, to humanize the country so that it can "perhaps" become the Holy Land. When does this process reach its last and definitive outcome? Never. As S. R. Hirsch has said, *"Gabe ist Aufgabe"* (gift is task). If the *"Aufgabe"* ceases to be, so does simultaneously the *"Gabe."* Everything Israel is or has must be conquered in an unceasing battle. The *telos* is in the struggling itself, for, quoting Blaise Pascal's Christ: "you would not be seeking me, had you not already found me." Or, in the words of Job, "though he slay me, yet will I trust in him." (13:15, KJV) Failure, that is to say, is the very condition for life: the vision of the promise necessarily implies suffering, defeat, nonfulfillment. A love without frustration is as dull as saccharine (as Rollo May would say). A life without obstacle is hell. This idea, which our modern societies are studiously at pains to forget—greatly damaging themselves in the process, e. g., through sex, violence, drugs—was better understood by the German Romantics when they stated *"Leben heisst kämpfen"* (life means to struggle). When we cease to strive in order to realize the promise, we *are* dead. A friend of mine told me about an uncle who, retired at the age of 65, spent the last years of his life watching television. Even his meals had to be brought to him at his place in front of the TV set. When he passed away, concluded my friend, he had already been dead for years.

It is thus clear that death—as well as all the obstacles in life which lead as premises to that last great failure—is no accident or chance. Death is therefore to be confronted; it is not to be ignored or prudishly veiled. Death does not come as the untimely negation of all that precedes, as the denial of all former affirmations in life. Rather, death is the outcome of love, for sacrifice *is* the very essence of love, i. e., of life. We become fully ourselves in dying for the sake of creating a "Thou," for the purpose of making room, all the room to the Other, divine or human. Thus, to the *tsimtsum* (contraction, shrinking, in the parlance of the Zohar) of God corresponds the *tsimtsum* of humanity. For the former it means that he discovers himself in his creatures, for the latter it means that we discover ourselves in God. As Abraham Heschel said, the Bible is both a theology for us and an anthropology for God.

Human liberty is one of the main questions Israel has to face. Here again, she proposes an answer of her own. It is a genuine and dialectical kind of response: human freedom is not any status we possess, human freedom consists of law. Faithful to her dynamic conception of reality, Israel does not speculate on any natural human quality called liberty. Such a status does not exist. Maimonides protests against the concept that liberty is native to us.[10] On the contrary, he says, in creating, God put his creature in the great danger of being at one with liberty, so that freedom would become our physical nature, instead of being a potentiality and an act. In that case, we would be determined by the constraint of being free! But freedom is a choice. In one of the most striking sayings of the Bible, Israel, facing Sinai, shouts *"NA'ASEH VE-NISHMA' "* (we will do, then we will heed; Exod. 24:7, my translation). The nature of liberty can only be revealed in existence, in the making. It is not any kind of possession. It is more a becoming than a being, more a process than an ontic quality. It is thus a process which anyone is free to disregard. This is why the so-called "Ten Commandments" open with an appeal to freedom, a plea to the people to (re)enact their liberty: " 'I am the LORD your God, who brought you out of the land of Egypt, out of the house of bondage. You shall. . . .' " (Exod. 20:2–3) The root of misunderstanding regarding the Torah in the Christian Church is the confusion constantly made between failure and unfeasibility. To be sure, nobody fulfills God's will—"there is not a righteous man on earth who does good and never sins" (Eccles. 7:20)—but that does not mean that God toys with us, confronting us with an impossible task. No father compels a three-year-old child to carry 100 pounds, or chastizes it because it cannot. The law of liberty contains a radical dimension of defeat. If not, the law *and* the liberty would be provisional, the will of God only relative, limited in time and in character. People fail to accomplish the Torah because they fail to accomplish their liberty. But, on the other hand, one cannot fail without being involved in the movement towards fulfillment. All of us go from defeat to defeat until the ultimate defeat—death; but in the process something eternal is made true in this life. Victory is in failure. Similarly, husband and wife learn through a lifespan that the triumph of their mutual love is embedded in the dynamism of the attempt to reach the unreachable. In the words of Rollo May, "The sex act is the most powerful enactment of relatedness imaginable. . . . It cannot be an accident of nature that in sex we thus enact the sacrament of intimacy and withdrawal, union and distance, separating ourselves and giving ourselves in full union again."[11] Paradoxically, an intimacy which would install itself and avoid withdrawal, distance, separation would kill love. Love without back-and-forth movement, of closeness and remoteness, love without the threatening possibility of its death or absence, is no love at all. Nobody can relate with a loving robot. If "God is love" (1 John 4:8), he must also be just and jealous and terrible and aggressive and murderous (cf. Gen. 22; Exod. 4:24ff.) and tormented (cf. Gen. 6:6; Exod. 32:14; 1 Sam. 15:11). That God is love means also that he meets with check, making himself dependent upon a response to his love, and who knows whether there will be a lover of God on earth? Nothing is more uncertain. But, conversely, the future is open, all is possible because humanity is free to make tomorrow different from today and yesterday. As a matter of fact, we have at our disposal the very means used by the Creator for giving birth to the heavens and the earth: love. In a universe where—Sartre is right so far—everything looks nonsensical, and where life seems nothing better than a tragicomedy, love is the unpredictable factor which changes the negative into the positive and transfigures failure into triumph.

This process of transfiguration—and it is precisely that, a process—is never complete. Life does not once and for all pass from a level of meaninglessness to one of meaning. Such a dualistic conception of life is not at home here. That which is meaningless must constantly be elevated into that which is meaningful. Between these polarities the distance is of course immense, the difference infinite; but such an evaluation is purely analytical, for, in essence, the omega toward which the alpha tends is itself nothing less than an alpha. Unceasingly, omega becomes a new alpha tending toward another omega, like heartbeats.

One clear illustration of the analytical distinction between these poles is provided by the primitive Church's introduction of a "delay of reflection" between Golgotha and Easter, while in fact the event of the cross and its value as "Easter" are simultaneous. It is characteristic of all failures to contain in themselves their "third day,"[12] their own transfiguration. In history as in nature there is no life but springing from death, no construction but on the basis of ruins. That is why Ernst Bloch can magnify the death in a concentration camp of a Communist, who has no recourse to any transcendence, whose death is not recompensed, but who nevertheless knows that his death is not meaningless.[13] The society of the year 2000 is grounded in his sacrifice. It is his free choice to prefer the creator's "death for something" to the parasite's "life for nothing." Seemingly, he is a "dead lion," while his Nazi torturers are "living dogs," but who could be so blind as not to see that the latter are "men of nothingness,"[14] whereas he *is* a man of plenitude? Bloch's hero exercises his free choice to become "eternal." He goes beyond himself. In doing so, he shares in the perennial plea of Israel.

There, in a history which triumphs over centuries and millennia, we witness an acceptance of death which is the opposite of suicide. From the origins to the end of time, people of all nations are the astonished spectators, moved or incredulous, of a sacrifice from which life flows unceasingly. Like the legendary phoenix, the historical Israel is born again from ashes. Losing her life, she gains it; dying out of love for God, the author of life, "it becomes impossible (according to the economy of love) that death retain her" (cf. Acts 2:24). Israel is the living, empirical confirmation that her existential choice of the *Aqedath Yitshak* (sacrifice of Isaac, Gen. 22), of the Servant's destiny (Isa. 53), of the cross, of Rabbi Akiba's martyrdom, and of Auschwitz[15] is paradoxically the source of life. When Frederick II asked his surgeon for a proof of the existence of God he got the reply: "The Jews, sire."

From the beginning, Israel received a terrible vocation: she was to make a total gift of herself. The Torah is actually the description of her true being, according to which she is no longer to be a slave to her desire for mortal power, and even for mere survival, but is freed to enjoy a life-giving communion with her God. Then, paradoxically, she lets die everything that from within and without constitutes a tie with negation and meaningless death. That is why the cross of Israel is fulfillment of the Torah. Without martyrdom, without self-sacrifice, without the failure of Auschwitz, the Torah is but a code of laws. A code of laws is meant for the protection of natural rights and primarily the right to existence. But Torah is no such expression of the natural law; it calls Israel to give the only positive response to God, that is, love heightened to the ultimate. Through it, finally, all people discover themselves in their integrity as creatures of God. In confronting all people with the Torah, Israel delivers them from idols, she demystifies them, and consequently she reveals to them what they are: free beings.

Such a conception of liberty is unique in religion and philosophy. It is, properly speaking, a *revelation.* I mean that, in facilitating a dynamic use of sovereign human choice, Israel reveals to all people their true selves. Confronted with a freedom which is "the choice of their being" and which transcends them so as to transfigure them into the image of God (Gen. 1:27) and to divinize them (2 Pet. 1:4; 2 Cor. 3:18), people have now escaped all bondages and are now able to be the creators they were expected to be since the beginning.[16]

That is how Israel is mediator. She does not possess a special, superhuman nature, but she reveals in her preaching and in her very existence the real nature of all people. She is a microcosm, an *imago hominum,* even as she is *imago Dei.* To rule out one of the two terms in mediation means that there is no more mediation, no more priesthood. The history of the "nations" only has meaning, real content, reality, in that of Israel. "The pagan nations will have to bow down, not only before Yhwh, but also before Israel (cf. Isa. 49:23; 43:3–4; 45:11–24). . . . The nations work to the profit of the chosen people."[17] For Israel is holy as her God is holy.

In Israel's conception, *holiness* is essentially dynamic. Human sanctity manifests Someone Else's sanctity. God alone is holy (cf. Isa. 40:25, and often in Second Isaiah; Hos. 11:9, etc.). God *is* holiness. *Qadosh* best expresses, according to Scriptures, God's being. In the words of Edmond Jacob, "The essential aspect of holiness is that of power, but of power . . . which communicates itself in order to bestow life."[18] It is therefore not a passive attribute of God but, on the contrary, the very activity of the one whose name is Yhwh, "I become with whom I become" (Exod. 3:14, my translation),[19] by which God reveals to Moses and the enslaved people in Egypt that His testing is bound up with theirs, that His becoming is embodied in Israel's. He creates *be-r'ešit,* in view of finding himself in humanity, and Israel becomes the quest of humanity for God. But, if this is true as far as human Israel is concerned, then *everyone* is potentially the incarnation of God's becoming. John 1:9 states: "The true light . . . enlightens every man." Before any response, before he was " 'formed . . . in the womb, God knew' " him (Jer. 1:5). He is chosen, he is consecrated, he is appointed (Jer. 1:5). The fact that only the prophet Jeremiah realizes in the sixth century that he is known by God, enlightened by true light and appointed for a mission of revelation, does not reduce the general to the particular. Jeremiah's destiny does not constitute a remarkable single experience. Jeremiah realizes his people's prophetic vocation and becomes for his nation the mirror of their prophetic dimension. Jeremiah, like all the representatives of *verus Israel,* is the demonstration that all people *qua* people are confronted with the primordial choice of becoming. All of life is a commentary on the Moment, even before birth, when we faced the ultimate and gave our response (cf. chapter 1 above).

Sartre is again right in saying that "every man must invent

his own way,"[20] but this invention is not random. It is the making of one's truth, the revelation of one's encounter with God. For God is not restricted to "heaven," and God's holiness is no remoteness from us as though he would jealously protect his divinity and remain in splendid isolation. The holiness of God is the energy of his relationship with us, his communication.

Since "holiness" in the Bible marks a separation, one must immediately add that God is separated *for*, not *from*. Separation here is dedication, commitment. That is why holiness is intimately linked to the covenant. God enters into covenant with people in order to give them what *he* is: "Be holy as I am holy." Thus, in the covenant, Israel passes from the category of the human to that of God. The humanization of God[21] brings about the human "sharing in God's being." (2 Pet. 1:4, my translation) To be sure, this does not mean that Israel takes the place of God and adopts his nature, but Israel becomes the action of God, his dynamism, the incarnation of the Name. "I am God, I am *not a man*, the holy one *in the midst of you.*" (Hos. 11:9, my translation; see Deut. 13:3; 30:11–14) For the strength of God, his positive difference, is the unalterable power he has to become feeble with us.

It is from this perspective of God's "weakness" that we can appraise the negative aspect of human liberty. For the *refusal* of the light which comes to "every man" (John 1:9) also belongs in a certain way to our freedom, but it is the freedom to murder freedom, it is license and chaos. "Man is not a fact but a becoming, not an act but a drama, not a nature but something to do, not a participle but a gerundive," says van der Leeuw.[22] We thus can do or undo our liberty. As we saw above, just as there is a positive death versus a negative death (and of course a positive existence versus a negative one), there is also a liberty to create, and a liberty to annihilate. The Maimonidian "command to be free" means that Israel has been called to reveal the authentic, positive, liberty to all. Light of the *goyim*, as Isaiah 42:6 says, the Jews are thus to become the archetypes for all. That this is a *call*, and not an innate Jewish virtue, is emphasized time and again by the very documents revered by the

Jews as "Holy Scriptures." Furthermore, there is in this nothing to be envied by other nations. One of my close Jewish friends, coming back from a German concentration camp, declared on his arrival home that he would gladly give up his life on the spot if this could prevent his son from being a Jew. But over and above every other dimension which makes individual Israelites just as "good" or as "bad" as any people among the Gentiles, there is also, there is above all, the dimension of their election. Whether or not they are willing to embrace it, it looks as if it "sticks" to them. They simply cannot get rid of it. Whenever they are about to, someone takes the terrible responsibility of recalling the fact to them and even of taking their lives because of it.[23]

The Jews' chosenness, their holiness as a nation, is no theoretical predicate. It is sacrifice. It is Auschwitz. To be envious of the Jews is to be naive or masochistic. If a nation wants to replace Israel, it will have to line up its citizens by millions for the crematoria. It is, as a matter of fact, a most tragic mistake —to which everyone is time and again exposed, the Christian in the first place—to confuse messianism with triumphalism. God, to be sure, is king, and he is calling his people to share in his kingship; but the way to it is love, suffering, and death. That is what the long history of Israel has been all about. The sanctification of the world depends upon the sanctification of Israel. Even as humanity is always "first" in creation, the Jews are always "first"—the New Testament says *proton*—in the economy of salvation. Let me again stress that this eminent function of Israel is not begotten by her pride. On the contrary, Israel is the first to recognize her insignificance and her natural incapacities. Israel *"kata sarka"*—as the New Testament again puts it —must unceasingly offer herself upon the altar of the Temple in order to be born anew according to her true image as presented to her by the Torah. The Israelites have their eyes fixed upon it in order to live in conformity with it, their authentic image. They identify themselves with it, investing their whole being in order to respond to their vocation of Word made flesh, of Torah made history, of "energy of the divine essence."

These last terms, which seem highly philosophical, sum up and emphasize the mystery of the fundamental difference between God's essence (transcendence) and energy (immanence). To say that Israel is the divine energy in the world is to repeat in other words the message of Exodus 3:14 which I have already discussed above. Israel's tie with the divine, Israel's holiness, is precisely that which binds her to the human. Nothing is truly human without divine dimension.[24] Neither is anything divine without human incorporation. As Dietrich Bonhoeffer put it: *"Einen Gott den es gibt, gibt es nicht"* (a god which there is, is not). For what would be such a god existing outside of the human becoming, outside of the human response which gives love its meaning? In fact, the "I" of God fills the "I" of Moses (cf. Exod. 3:12 and 13; note the double emphasis on the word *"anochi"*="I" as used by God and by Moses), and Israel lives the duality of this "I" in which the marriage between Creator and creature is fulfilled. Their unity is dual and begets the tension between the two poles of their covenant, as between male and female in the duality of their being-one-flesh. True, the tension is towards the reduction of the duality, but the tension is without end; it does not degenerate into the static swallowing of one by the other, but they find together their *pleroma* in the birthing of a common action for God and for humanity.

Thus the tension between the two extremes is eternal. It is this movement, this very tension which is the encounter. No equilibrium is ever possible between the human animal and the divine. If there is a thread in between, it must necessarily come to the point of breaking. And the sons of God die on crosses because "to love God [is] . . . for man a level of experience he can only reach at the price of his death."[25]

If therefore Israel finds herself in a privileged situation at the heart of humanity, this eminence is no quality of hers, it is an *action*. It is no status but a continuous victory over herself. In this respect, there is no more concrete test for her sanctifying activity than the very ground on which she stands. As is well known, Jewish tradition situates Israel's homeland at the heart of the earth. Now we might see this as just another fiction comparable to the great many claims made all over the world, especially in primitive myth, for the centrality of this or that particular nation,[26] were it not for the fact that the notion of "centrality" in Israel is based not on a given geographical or mythical status but rather on the historical action which *makes* the land central, and holy. (I shall return to this difficult point in a forthcoming book dealing with God and Auschwitz.)

Placed at the center of the cosmos, Israel is its principle of sanctification; she is the leaven which causes the impetuousness of life in the amorphous and static dough. She is the "germ," the assurance of the fertility of creation. The germ acts from near to near, transforming in itself all that is foreign. It unites in itself all that is dispersed. So does Israel "dominate" nature (cf. Gen. 1:28)—leading it towards its final fulfillment according to the Creator's design, taking all the responsibility for its evolution, "cultivating and keeping it" as a "gardener" (see Gen. 2:15).

Nothing makes this return of nature to its "supernaturality" more real than the *koshruth,* the ritual purity of the priestly food. For eating is an act of communion. In their relationship with nature, people have only two alternatives, either to worship nature and be absorbed by it through appropriate rites, or to "historicize" it by making it participate in their becoming through incorporating its life-giving products. When doing the latter, they magnify both themselves and nature; it is a communion of life to which all people and the whole of creation are invited. When food is shared, life is shared. Meal sharing actualizes and affirms one's fellowship and communion with others and, ultimately, with God. To eat is to interiorize. That is why Jewish literature and tradition see the act of absorbing foods as similar to sexual union. Accordingly, the verb "to eat" in the Bible sometimes has a metaphorical sense.[27] It is to be noted that the Hebrew word for "table" means in fact altar. To sit around the table for a meal is therefore the gathering of the community around God for sharing with him the substance of creation. It is a sacrifice—and in this connection it must be stressed that the consumption of the remaining parts of a litur-

gical sacrifice is an integral part of the offering. During the
meal, God, people, and the whole of creation are present. It is
a cosmic act, a cosmic liturgy of worship and communion.
Thanks to the commonality of what the divine and human partners share together during the meal-sacrifice, they actually
meet on a common ground. Any quid pro quo is avoided; any
disincarnated mysticism excluded.

Such a "leveling" of the partners of the dialogue is far-
reaching. It is also revolutionary with regard to the conception
of priesthood in Israel. For, whereas the priests of other nations
are in fact a caste of people maintaining jealously the esoteri-
cism of their wisdom and of their power in the image of their
divinities' remoteness, Israel's priests are representative of the
priesthood of the whole people, as we saw in chapter 3. The
heathen priests are sorcerers, magicians, disposing of a sacred
trust which invests them with supernatural powers. They handle magic, and this distinguishes them from all others in the
tribe or the nation. Moreover, they have received by tradition
an external corpus of knowledge which remains foreign to humanity *per se*. Because theirs is a nonhuman wisdom it super-
venes upon merely human wisdom; the priests handle powerful
items but they themselves are not existentially committed to
them. They are not, in their souls, transformed by them; they
are merely technicians.

In Israel, to the contrary, the priest receives only a *delega-
tion*. We have seen that every male in Israel is a priest in full
right; he is *redeemed* from his public priesthood by the Levites
who substitute for the whole people. Their office does not con-
fer upon them a superhuman status of any kind, for to be in the
vicinity of the sacred means in fact to be exposed to death. No
one can see God and live. The parallel drawn, by Exodus 13 for
instance, between the death of the firstborn in Egypt and the
redemption of the firstborn in Israel through the institutionalized priesthood is striking in this respect.

A priest "to the tip of her fingers,"[28] Israel speaks a holy
language. To be sure, it is a human language with dimensions
perfectly congruent with those of other Semitic languages, but

it is distinguished nevertheless from all others in that it attempts to shape all of its words so as to make them express a basic relational meaning in the framework of the covenant with God. In this perspective, Hebrew claims to call all things by their proper names, i. e., by the word which reveals their identity. In a universe conceived as the meeting place of vocational beings, it is of course essential that the true personality of the partners be revealed in language. The Hebrew noun is a dynamic description of a particular action which belongs properly to the uniqueness of a person or thing. Whereas our Indo-European languages are content with affixing labels as designations of objects, Hebrew, by contrast, conceives itself as a prophetic plea to everything and everyone to become a subject. This is made possible by attributing to them not a conventional noun but a *name* conveying their inner potentiality, their existential tension towards their definite fulfillment. Here, therefore, words are not inflated in order to lift them up to the religious realm. The first meaning of "table" does not designate the common, contingent, profane object, and then only secondly, through a conventional process, a "holy Table" in use in a sacred space by special people at uncommon times. "Table" in Hebrew points first and above all to the *altar*, the place for the supper with God (cf. Ezek. 39:20; Num. 4:7; Mal. 1:7, etc.). Here the objects have a vocation, a priestly function, in their relation to God and consequently to humanity. No word is profane. There is *no* dualism between a realm of God and another realm of humanity. Human work *(abodah)* is above all worship, divine service and *therefore* so is any human creative activity.[29]

On the level of language or of activity, therefore, there is a correspondence between the earth and the heavens.[30] The *abodah* of humanity is echoing the one of God, both are the obverse and the reverse of the same reality. God and his human creatures are married. They have become one, with one shared creative activity through one shared language. They can have their own proper discourses *(debarim)* but these are in harmony with each other *(ahadim)* because their language is common *(saphah ahath)*.[31] There is in such mutuality, however, always one proviso; namely, that we do not reverse the terms of the relation. We are God's image, not conversely. Our work is the echo of God's creative and redemptive activity, not the other way round. The Jews are not worshiping their own inventiveness, their own history. For humanity is also able to debase God's work. The correspondence of heavens and earth is dynamic, not automatic.

It is thus striking to notice that on the level of Biblical vocabulary as well, it is God who comes down towards people and not they who go up towards God. All other languages have to transpose their vocabulary, made on the human scale, in order to address their divinities. Hebrew is the "language of the holy, or of holiness." "There," says Marcel Jousse, "the style comes from the whole man and goes to the whole man."[32] When, for example, Greek-speaking Jews in Alexandria were translating the Hebrew Scriptures into their vernacular language, they found themselves confronted with a recurrent problem. Hebrew words had no Greek equivalent, not only, as is common when passing from one culture to another, because of an expected "horizontal" difference of connotation between cognates of two languages, but because the difference was as it were "vertical." Greek words were pointing to concepts, pure ideas, belonging to an "intelligible world" with which words had intrinsically nothing in common.[33] Hebrew words on the contrary attempted to "adhere" to things, to "ex-press" reality, to make known the soul of the matter. There was no dissociation between the thought and its expression, between the people and their words. *Dabar* (word) in Hebrew expresses a vital flux coming from the innermost heart of the speaker. When God or his mandatory (priest, prophet) speaks, he draws from his "back,"[34] from his innermost, the exposition of his identity. The priestly word is therefore not an opinion but an incursion, an interpellation, an invocation: it forces into dialogue. As Edmond Jacob says, the Word does not merely interpret events it creates them.[35] The priestly speakers are fully committed, they throw themselves along with their discourses into the historical process. The Word is event. It does not simply describe, but pro-

vokes, instigates, stirs up. It gives shape to the unknown or to
the undreamed of. Saying that the people will go into exile in
Babylon is to make the future event pass from the realm of the
inconceivable into that of the factual, from nothingness into
being. There is nothing magical in such a conception, however.
For Israel, when a word is really ex-pressing the truth—i. e., the
essence of history, its oriented dynamism—the word belongs to
that truth, is part of that dynamism. It *names* the event, it says
its content, its rationale, its purpose, inasmuch as this language
of worship can designate the real place things occupy in their
historical relationship with God and humanity.

In the chaos of human languages, the priestly language itself
is an event. It is the event of discerning and creating, of bringing into the world the creative order of the Word. No doubt
such a means of communication does not stand on the level of
the "mass media." It is no transitory, conventional, accidental
tool in the hands of Israel. It is, on the contrary, an integral part
of the vocation of the chosen people. It is a dimension in the
sanctification of the created. Without the priestly "language of
the holy," human languages are but confused sounds without
reality. Or rather, they are vain attempts to express a reality
always elusive and forever beyond reach. They are pathetic,
"barbaric" rumblings for uttering the ultimate.

As for Israel, all of her life, all of her action, all of her becoming tends towards the moment when the microcosm will become macrocosm, when the will of God will be accomplished
on earth as it is in heaven. The expression of this tension is called
the Torah, for which life is authentic only when it is totally
sanctified and priestly. True, it is explicitly addressed to Israel
as a people, as the sociological-religious community involved in
the coordinates of time-history and space-geography. But it is
also God's plea to all people to become Israel, to become
human. Not only has the Torah been presented to all nations,
according to the rabbis, but the exegesis of the latter on Genesis
1:26–27 is potently far-reaching in this respect. To be sure, they
affirm that the similitude with the divine is true for every
human being, but in fact only the Israelites—no racial connota-

tion intended—are the *imago Dei*, for only they have chosen to live according to the Mosaic Law. In doing so, they identify themselves with God who in the first place complies with his own Torah.[36]

These are the constituting elements of *holy history*—that is to say a history which sanctifies itself by sanctifying—in tension towards the *Kairos*, towards the privileged moment in which all the other moments recognize their true image, the moment when holiness is accomplished.

5. | The Messianic People

Does Israel accomplish her vocation?

This question, raised repeatedly within a skeptical Christendom, is almost always merely rhetorical: the expected answer is that Israel, historically and spiritually, has simply missed the point. The Synagogue, according to a familiar stereotype, struggles vainly to reach a goal (a *telos*) which has been achieved independently of her by "Jesus Christ," rendering her efforts pathetic and finally without meaning or significance. The wheels of the Jewish carriage turn in the void. Like new, tragic heirs of Sisyphus, the Jews are denied any significant, any decisive work. Their presence among us is anachronistic, unless, like the Middle Ages, we accord them the negative value of being witnesses to the Christians—the new people of God—of the wrath of the Lord. Israel is then a sad and potent living example of what could happen—God forbid!—to the Church if she betrayed her faithfulness.

To be sure, it is easy enough to arraign the Jewish people on endless charges. The demonstration of their sinfulness is within the reach of anyone. The indictment is inexorably provided by Jewish Scriptures themselves. Not so long ago, the Nazis impudently used this self-criticism of Israel's tradition to point out the Jews' "wickedness." In so doing, they simply prolonged a trend present in Christianity almost since its inception. And indeed, that Israel participates in the human rebellion against God is no invention or discovery of the Christian establishment. No people are less complacent with themselves than the Jews, for they know very well that their priestly task in a way never reaches the goal. They know that in the course of her history, in the movement of her becoming, Israel tends to settle. They experience in their bones and flesh the *failure* inherent in their history. The accomplishment is always *beyond,* always before them, never behind. To no one more than to the Jews does the striving toward fulfillment appear vain, hopeless, ludicrous. The *telos* seems to be receding faster than they can possibly proceed towards it. It may even appear to them that their very efforts at grasping the eschaton repel it further on. Their God is a terrible God, simultaneously known and unknown, whose truth is a bottomless abyss. No people on earth have ever had a more dramatic conception of their relationship with the Divine. Thus, those who are daring enough to plunge into it must, like Kierkegaard, commit themselves in advance to a leap into the void. Who knows whether they will be harbored in the bosom of God? Who knows whether they will succeed in passing through the bloody pieces of the beasts divided in the midst (Gen. 15, my translation), when "the sun goes down and a thick darkness comes," when they are confronted with the "smoking furnace and the flaming torch" of Auschwitz? Abraham issued alive and purified out of the melting pot of the encounter with God, but what about his brother Nahor, who, according to the Jewish Midrash, exposed himself to the burning stake at Ur in imitation of Abraham, but was consumed? What about Lot? What about Lot's wife? And what about Eliezer of Damascus who shared in his master's destiny and for this reason lost his heritage in favor of Isaac? For whenever people come near to God, they must sometime, somehow, in their own way, sacrifice their only son, and wrestle with the angel until their name, their soul, is changed in the process . . . in the name of *Hope.*

It is true that, in the words of William the Silent, "it is not necessary to hope in order to undertake, nor to succeed in order to persevere," but William was using here the term "hope" with the meaning of speculation as to feasibility. And, indeed, it is not "necessary" for a person—or for God—to be sure of the victory. It is enough to live in the "maybe," for the latter is the very foundation of liberty. The failure inherent in the "perhaps" makes us free to *choose* and *therefore* to fail. As Neher says, "the liberty of man is the radical factor of uncertainty."

Thus, when the primitive Church comes to the revolutionary conclusion that Jesus of Nazareth has been *made* Lord and Messiah by God (Acts 2:36), such a confession of faith needs to be carefully examined and rightly understood. Obviously, the claim was based on the "resurrection" (cf. 1 Cor. 15) and on the related conviction that the Nazarene had "accomplished all" (cf. John 19:30). Those who confessed Jesus as "living," "resurrected," were Jews, representatives precisely of the only people on earth who dared to assume failure and to proclaim that victory is not beyond defeat but *in* defeat.[1] This very fact sheds a new light on the whole matter and first of all on the delay introduced by the New Testament texts between the death and resurrection of "Christ."[2] Such a gap of three days between the two occurrences has led the Gentile Christians to the wrong conclusion that the events are more or less independent of each other. In certain of the Hellenized communities founded by Paul, some were sharing in the eucharist in remembrance only of Jesus' resurrection, and Paul had to remind them that "as often as you eat this bread and drink the cup, you proclaim the Lord's death until he comes." (1 Cor. 11:26) At least three reasons dictated the literary and theological device of placing the resurrection on a Sunday, three days after the death on the cross. First, the disciples had felt a deep despair at the sight of their assassinated master. They readily concluded that they had been mistaken in following him and in hoping in his glorification. It was only later that they came to the opposite conviction that the martyr had been made Lord and Messiah. They therefore projected their own hesitation in time and introduced a gap between death and resurrection.[3] They did this because they were not speaking objectively of the events but expressing their own faith and their own conversion from despair to comfort. In the same manner the prophets during the exile in Babylon spoke of restoration as following up the actual dereliction of Israel, at the same time making it clear that the *galuth* itself did not mean only banishment but also and above all revelation.[4]

The latter is simultaneous with the former, but the *consciousness* of it comes only later.

Second, the symbolism of the "three days" is a deeply rooted pattern in Israel. It conveys an idea akin to the myths of passage in the heathen religions. Joshua 1:11 alludes to a three-day preparation for the crossing of the Jordan. Jonah remains three days and three nights in the fish's belly (2:1; see 3:3 with the same symbolism); Esther bids the Jews not to eat or drink for three days; Jesus promises to rebuild the Temple in three days (Mark 14:58; John 2:19). Above all, the theophany is bound with "the third day" (Exod. 19:11, 15, 16; Hos. 6:2; cf. 1 Sam. 3:8). Hence, it is clear that the statement about the resurrection of Jesus occurring on "the third day" is not an objective one, it is kerygmatic, apologetic: the destiny of the Nazarene reenacts the great theophany on Mount Sinai (cf. Mark 9:31; Luke 24: 21).[5]

Third, one can infer that Sunday has been chosen for either one or all of the following reasons. The insistence of the texts upon the crucifixion taking place *before* the sabbath is striking (cf. Mark 16:1–2; Matt. 28:1; Luke 24:1). Obviously nothing new could possibly occur before the sabbath was over, i. e., at the earliest on the first day of the following week. Moreover, practically, the first Christians met with the other Jews in the Temple for celebrating the sabbath. The whole day was dedicated to rest and meditation. They shared with their fellow Jews this respect. When the day was over, i. e., on the evening of the Saturday, the Christians in fact "prolonged" the sabbath with their own particular eucharistic meetings. They did this the more easily as only one day in the week besides the sabbath had prominence over the others: the first, because of its very place in the week. By placing the resurrection on Sunday, they made clear that Christ is the beginning of a new era, the initiator of the New Covenant. It is even a possibility that the mystic speculations among the Jews on the "eighth day" already existed at the time. If so, the Christians proclaimed, by calling the "first day of the week" (Matt. 28:1; Mark 16:2, 9; Acts 20:7; 1 Cor. 16:2) the "day of the Lord" (Acts 2:20; 1 Cor. 1:8; 5:5; 2 Cor.

1:14), that the imperfection of the "seventh day" had opened on the perfect sabbath of the eight day.[6]

Furthermore, the resurrection day was a secondary motif, as is borne out by the fact that Mark, for example, attempts to minimize or even to eliminate that milestone on the way from crucifixion to parousia. True, the resurrection is affirmed through the discovery of the empty tomb (Mark 16:1ff.), but the appearances of the resurrected Christ are not mentioned and so there is continuity between the death and the final glorification of the Son of Man.

Be that as it may, it is an inevitable conclusion that the delay between Good Friday and Easter must not be taken literally. The far-reaching bearing of this is that the resurrection is *in* the crucifixion, the triumph is *in* the ultimate defeat. Faith and hope have not been superseded by the sights and "the ringing bells of Easter." The chips are not down and never will be. The resurrection of Jesus is no static verification of fact but "a leap in the void," as it was for the primitive Church and for Kierkegaard. Nobody has ever seen with fleshly eyes the empty tomb; but faith is no vague yearning, it is "the assurance of things hoped for, the conviction of things not seen." (Heb. 11:1) Those who love *see* (assurance, conviction, certitude) the triumph of their love. For them—and they are absolutely right—the fulfillment of their relationship with the beloved is more certain than $1+1=2$, but it is an existential assurance, an assurance made for them and not they for the assurance. They see the empty tomb because they empty the tomb of meaninglessness. "Christ is risen" means that we are fulfilled and glorified only in our own ultimate sacrifice. In this sacrifice of ourselves, we are, for the first time, at one with ourselves, we cleave to our identity.

To speak of *our* accomplishment apropos of Jesus' resurrection is no abusive broadening of the issue. It is the issue. The "Christian" process of mythologization of Jesus has made of him a hero, a half-man half-God personage. Faith in him has become an adherence to an objective and foreign spectacle with God, Jesus, and maybe the devil on the stage. Faith consists in applauding the right party, and then going home with a good conscience, reassured on the score of one's generosity.

Such a myth has been engendered by, among other things,
the misconception of the "once for all" of the epistle to the
Hebrews (cf. 9:26, 27, 28, etc.). It is easy from our point of view
to conceive of Christ as acting in a once-and-for-all completed
drama. But if we do that, then we today, and the people of the
past 2000 years, are mere spectators of a self-contained, definitive tragedy. We are not part of it. Our history comes "too late"
and has no decisive bearing upon *"Heilsgeschichte."* We are, as
theological systems put it, at the benefit of grace, i. e., of something that happened without us and that requires from us primarily our intellectual adherence.

But this way, all subsequent developments after Golgotha
are reduced to the rank of minor happenings, and even a formidable event such as Auschwitz, presenting such potent parallels
with Calvary, finds no place in "Christian" reflection as such. At
best, it is a terrible accident demonstrating human wickedness.
Our attention is focused on the German monsters, and we do
not know what we are to do theologically with the Jewish martyrdom. How does it make any sense? Or is the death of six
million Jews because they were "Semite*s*" (a word which means
"carriers of the Name") a meaningless event? Is it tenable for
"Christians" today to continue to speak pathetically of the torture of the Innocent of Nazareth and ignore the Calvary of the
six million innocents at Nazi hands? Do we need experts for
measuring the comparative degree of innocence, of suffering,
of acceptance, of resignation between Jesus and his brethren of
the twentieth century? Do we not see that it is exactly the *same*
Event which continues from alpha to omega? Abraham and
Isaac in Moriah, the Jewish martyrs under Antiochus IV (Epi-
phanes), Jesus on the cross, Rabbi Akiba on the stake, the six
million of God's children in the crematoria—all are the Suffering Servant of the Lord realizing that there exists no other way
to love God than to give up one's life: " 'Greater love has no
man than this, that a man lay down his life for his friends.' "
(John 15:13) More than life no one can give, for to give one's life
is to give all one has.[7]

"All is accomplished" says Jesus on the cross, according to the primitive Church. Yes, all is fulfilled in the sacrifice to God. All are then themselves; all discover their true identity. For, someday, somehow, in some way, I shall be brought to break open my innermost. I shall have to spell out my truth, the truth of my being, my soul. I shall say my very own version of the Name of God, bringing forth the fulfillment of my vocation, the accomplishment of my *raison d'être*. And when this unique Word of mine is uttered, there will be no return to my former mediocrity, because my Word will consume the totality of my being, like the flame emanating from the log in the hearth. For that moment I was born; that moment alone gives the ultimate meaning to all preceding events of my life. This at last is Me. All the rest is a rough draft. As the Baal Shem Tov about to die (in 1760) said: "Now I know for what purpose I was created."

When the Nazarene on the cross "let out a *phone megale*" before expiring (Mark 15:37, my translation), it was more than "a loud cry"! He then uttered his ultimate Word; he pronounced the Name which is above all names, as the high priest does at Yom Kippur in the Holy of Holies.[8] Hence, "the curtain of the Holiest was rent in two from top to bottom" (Mark 15:38, my translation) as a sign of the extension of the holy to the confines of the profane (cf. Zech. 14:20–21). For the event of the cross was not a private affair between Joshua the Nazarene and God, but a *human* response, a response of the human to God. Its all-inclusive humanness—for it was no more foreign to anyone than one's own death is—became the human rejoinder of love to the love of God. Thus, Israel showed again that the authentic human act is love. This is our work, our *abodah*, our worship, our accomplishment. The primitive Church had nothing else to say but that: when we go down to the tomb for the love of God, in fact the tomb is empty. "God raises us up, having loosed the pangs of death, because it is not possible for us to be held by it" (cf. Acts 2:24). Nothing has power over love, not even death. The Jewish faith in resurrection is based on nothing reducible to logical, scientific formulas. It is a cry against all evidence, the discovery of the greatest mystery, the *creation* of truth. The disciples' flashing intuition has been to designate the all-concrete peasant of Nazareth as the Risen One. Precisely he who "had no form nor comeliness, that we would look upon him; nor beauty that we should delight in him" (cf. Isa. 53:2, KJV), he who was condemned as a vulgar agitator and criminal, has been *made* Lord and Christ. In him, not in any powerful potentate, the choosing and the messianic vocation of Israel have been brought to fulfillment. That is why what is said of Israel in the "Old Testament" is, quite simply, applied to Christ in the New.[9]

An example of this identification pertaining particularly well to our present work is the argument in Hebrews that Jesus Christ is the priesthood of Israel (cf. 4:14; 7:26). The demonstration pivots around the idea of accomplishment. In Christ Israel meets her fulfilled commission to be the "kingdom of priests" for the world. In order to make its case, Hebrews calls upon the mysterious figure of Melchizedek. This personage coming from Genesis 14 and Psalm 110 is especially interesting in that he is the priest of a non-Israelite people and, therefore, symbolically the priest of all non-Jews in the time of Abraham. Abraham— himself a symbol of the Jewish people to come from his loins— thus meets in the person of Melchizedek a representative of the Noachic covenant. The implication is that the latter maintains within a world cut off from God a priestly order "after the manner of Melchizedek" (Ps. 110:4, my translation), capable of sparing the world a catastrophe similar to that during the time of Noah. For, if God has promised never again to destroy the earth, it does not mean that henceforth he will close his eyes to the "threefold and even fourfold crime" of every nation under the sky (cf. Amos 1—2). Rather, it means that he brings up out of the nations priests such as Melchizedek or Jethro, righteous men such as Job, pure hearts such as Rahab or Ruth.[10] These "pagan saints of the Old Testament"—to quote Father Jean Danielou—are Israel's presence where they live, and have their definite value because mysteriously they are connected with Israel. This truth becomes conspicuous to themselves and to

everyone the very moment they come in contact with their
"source." Only when Melchizedek meets Abraham; only when
Jethro meets Moses; Tamar, Judah; Rahab, the Israelite spies;
Ruth, Naomi—only then is their destiny fulfilled and they are
able to name the God they only knew intuitively. Being in the
Noachic covenant, they discover the emergence of their economy into the economy of Abraham, for, although coming later
chronologically, the relationship of God with Abraham is nevertheless "first" and constitutes the very foundation of the alliance with Noah. The world is under the protection of God
because and on behalf of Abraham. The Jewish literature affirms
with its customary insight that it is in view of Abraham that the
world was created.[11]

Conversely, the multiple sin of humanity, as denounced for
example by Amos, finds its origin and its condition in the fact
that Judah and Israel have committed a disobedience—whose
mildness, it is true, seems incommensurate with the genocides
perpetrated by the nations. The former and the latter are, however, put on the same level of responsibility because the people
of Israel are "the only ones that God has known out of all the
families of the ground. That is why God shall hold an accounting
against them for all their iniquities." (Amos 3:2, my rendering;
cf. 1:1—2:3; 2:4–16) If the priest sins, what will the nations do?

It is therefore an exceptionally serious mistake to see the
letter to the Hebrews in general, and chapter 7 of it in particular, as creating a schism between a restricted covenant—that
with Israel in Abraham, Isaac, and Jacob—and a far larger covenant called "the order of Melchizedek," with all people. The
author of Hebrews does not separate Abraham and Melchizedek. On the contrary, he shows their relationship. Abraham
bows before Melchizedek and receives his blessing. The epistle
comments at this point that "the inferior is blessed by the superior" (7:7), again leaving no doubt that Abraham and Melchizedek represent in Genesis 14 much more than themselves. Two
priesthoods face each other, the Levitical and the universal.
The former is the condition of the latter but gives place to it
once it appears. Even before Israel becomes the priestly leaven

of the dough of the world, Abraham is the witness of Melchizedek, bread that is raised and ready to be eaten, wine that is
drawn and ready to be drunk.

Before Israel's history actually starts, its fulfillment is already
present! For the accomplishment is not to be found in a chronological end after the historical process. It is *in* the process and
even before the process has become visible or conscious (cf. Isa.
49:1–2, 5; Jer. 1:5; Matt. 1:20–23, etc.). Before any action on the
part of humanity, God has already accomplished all things.
What this means is certainly not that history is of no avail, or
comes "too late" as Oscar Cullmann says,[12] everything being in
any case already done by God. But just as it is true that the
whole of one's existence is already present—"telescoped"—in
the embryo; just as it is true that love is not the outcome of a
pre-love process but exists or does not exist at all; just as it is true
that the revelation of God is not progressive as if "God" were
a philosophical truth to be understood better and better—revelation is rather the full gift of himself since the beginning—it is
also true that the *telos* is present and reached with the beginning. The eschaton is not only before us but behind us and
constantly with us. Abraham faces it and bows down before it.
The primitive Church makes Jesus say: " 'Your father Abraham
rejoiced that he was to see my day; he saw it and was glad.' "
(John 8:56) At this point, look back at chapter 2 and its discussion of the word *r'ešit* (beginning, or rather "prime") in Genesis
1:1; the narrative on creation is actually eschatological.

Hebrews 7:12, 18–19, 22, etc. therefore in no way minimizes
or relativizes the Torah of Moses. The sacred author is addressing the Jews—and Jews would never have followed him on the
terrain that some people nowadays believe they discover in
these texts. His aim is to put the Law and the covenant of the
Hebrew Scriptures back into their true eschatological perspective. Far from despising them because of the coming of "the
high priest" according to the order of Melchizedek, he sees
them as opening out on their universal accomplishment of the
salvation of the world (that is what Melchizedek represents).
That which was relative (to the coming of an era of perfection)

reveals itself also as absolute (the salvation of all creation in the person of the high priest offering up himself, 7:27). It is a new underlying era, in the Biblical sense of the word. That is to say that the "old" era finds in the "new" its final blossoming. Indeed, with the exception of a few very precise cases (as Eccles. 1:9: "nothing new under the sun"), the term "new" must be understood in the sense of "renewed." The new covenant is a renewed covenant, always the same, but having attained its *telos*. A new heart is the heart which has gone through the renewal of itself. New birth is not an additional birth but the recapitulation on a transfigured level of one's life. The priesthood of Israel is renewed in Christ, according to the epistle to the Hebrews, because he is the high priest of all humanity.[13]

It is a mistake to seek in the humble attitude of Abraham as contrasted with Melchizedek's glory the prefiguration of the "humiliation of the Synagogue." Abraham is chosen from the midst of a family, a people, all people, *in order to* bring to the end of creation the heavenly blessing (Gen. 12:3). The dynamism of his history is fully expressed in his vocation which contains its own end (its accomplishment, its *pleroma,* and consequently its relativity). Melchizedek presents himself to Abraham as the living reminder that the very movement of the work of Israel cannot be valid in itself. A movement without an arrival at its end would be a disguised stasis. Abraham, movement personified (see Gen. 12:1), bows down before the prefiguration of its destination. For Melchizedek has neither beginning nor end, being in person the All, the All accomplished (cf. Heb. 7:13). He is the king of Salem, the king of peace in the Biblical sense of the term (Heb. 7:2), the king of totality, of wholeness, of integrity before God. His order is not temporary (limited in its origin by initial movement and in its end by a new era). It is not in need of receiving its sense from any superior order.

As for Abraham, he needs the omega point because without this his adventure would be absurd. Melchizedek is not the river which throws itself into the ocean; he himself is the ocean. Abraham therefore bows down before the one who, "without father, without mother, without genealogy, has neither begin-

ning of days nor end of life, but resembles the Son of God."
(Heb. 7:3, my translation) He kneels before the one who is more
Abraham than he is himself.

Israel also must bow down before the final accomplishment
of herself. Not, to be sure, someone separable from Israel but
someone who, like the Servant of the Lord in Isaiah, is distinct
and indistinct from her. Distinct in that he, and he alone, is
what the nation was not able or did not want to be (cf. Isa. 53:6);
indistinct in that his sacrifice *is* that of the whole people (cf. Isa.
53:4, 11, 12, etc.).

From this perspective, it is to be noted that, in the opinion
of the epistle to the Hebrews, God chose the high priest according to the order of Melchizedek in his very people! To raise him
up out of the "nations," would have been to suppress with one
stroke of the pen the whole *"Heilsgeschichte,"* the covenant
itself, the whole commitment of God since the beginning. But
no such thing took place. The priest according to the order of
Melchizedek is the supreme representative of the priestly nation.

They must find their accomplishment, their perfect stature
in the priesthood of one of their representatives. The priesthood of Israel as such is not suppressed, nor is it diminished. But
all priesthood is then manifestly—and it has always been so in
hope—*in relation with,* and related to, the high priesthood of
the one who recapitulates the whole priestly work of his people
in the past as well as in the future. For the priesthood of Israel
is like the cone of a mountain. Whether one looks down on the
left face or on the right face, it is still the same mountain.
Whether one speaks of the period before Christ or the period
after Christ, it is still the same priesthood. In hailing Joshua the
Nazarene as Israel's high priest, the primitive Church saw personified in him Israel's holiness,[14] Israel's work, past, present,
and future.[15]

Jesus, the man from Nazareth in Galilee, is therefore inseparable from his people whose existence and history he fills with
his own life and passion. Cut off from Israel, he is but a dreamer,
a shadow, the absurdity and distress of a verb with neither

subject nor object. He is nothing. It is together *with* the messianic people, of which he incarnates the messiahship, that he gives to his work the infinite extension of the framework of holiness. All the earth is the Lord's; all the families of the earth bless themselves by Abraham; all peoples go up to the mountain of the Lord, to the house of the God of Jacob, and they accompany the Jew for they have heard that God is with him (cf. Zech. 8:23). Holiness, like a river, does not leave its Israelite bed in order to open another, international one. The river overflows, it floods the earth, but it still follows its course, because it is eternal. Henceforth the whole earth becomes the holy land, because the central land stretches itself to the limits of the world; every language becomes a holy language because it rediscovers its point of reference in the "language of the holy"; every person becomes holy because every one joins the people of Israel; all food is *kosher* because all food enters into the sphere of the *koshruth;* all existence is holy because it is placed under the light which lightens Israel from the beginning. All that had to be accomplished by Israel (Jesus solemnly pronounces the *"dei,"* one must) is being accomplished. The concentric circles have reached the "islands," the confines of all creation, of the whole creature. Their center was, is, and will remain Zion.[16]

Jesus, "the Central Jew," conforms himself, needless to say, to this prophetic vision. He "limits" his ministry to the twelve tribes,[17] teaches in the Temple, identifies his body with the latter, suffers, and dies in Jerusalem. In relationship to Zion the movement therefore is centripetal. In coming in, the nations rediscover their center of gravity, their navel, the bond of all their members, without which they would be scattered to the winds (cf. Ezek. 37:2, 7*b*). This is why the gospel begins by showing the wise men of the Orient gathering around the Bethlehem manger. In John 7, Jesus cries in the Temple of Jerusalem: " 'If any one thirst, let him come to me and drink. He who believes in me, as the scripture has said, "Out of his heart shall flow rivers of living water," ' " thereby showing during the feast of the tabernacles that he is the Rock out of which this water flows.[18] Jesus then proceeds to the purification of the Temple (Matt. 21; John 2):

> Even as Yhwh brings the world to its second birth from the Temple, Jesus made his entry into the Temple in order to transform the world and inaugurate the messianic times in the very center of Israel and the world. This had to take place in Israel and only in Israel for the sake of the remnant of Israel—but precisely for this reason, solely for this reason, this had consequences for the whole world. . . . The mission of Jesus, the Messiah, is the cosmic transformation which can be effected only from the axis of the cosmos: Israel. . . . Jesus considered his relationship with the pagans in the vertical dimension of the perspective of the history of redemption. He was "universalist" *precisely because, only because,* he was "particularist." From the spring on the mountain of Zion, from the center, the streams of the waters of redemption flow in all directions, flow towards the "others" who will be the new people. In Jerusalem, the Son of Man gives his life as a ransom for many (Matt. 20:28). The Son of Man dies at Jerusalem, at the center.[19]

The apostle Paul underlines this "centrality" even in the new economy. For example, in Romans 15:19 (my translation) he writes that he spread the gospel "from Jerusalem and starting from the center of a circle, describing a periphery even into Illyricum." Also, as is well known, he reports "to the Twelve" about his "eccentric" activities. But above all, we must here note the collection he organizes for the "saints at Jerusalem." Besides, the words "poor" and "saints" are technical terms for designating the first Church in Jerusalem. The collection on their behalf, as Sundkler has shown, was rather a tax which the mother assembly, on that very basis, had the right to demand of the pagan converts (compare especially 1 Cor. 16:1ff. and 2 Cor. 1:12ff.).

Let me quote, from this perspective, the following conclusion of the same author:

> According to primitive Christian opinion, the initial mission of the apostles was to remain in Jerusalem, and not

to cover the world. The eyes of the apostles were turned
to the One who is to come, and so it was imperative at
the last moment to put the remnant of Israel in safety in
the community of Christ and to make it the house and
the Church of Israel. This could only be done in Jerusalem (Acts 1:4). . . . The essential denouement of the
drama having taken place in Jerusalem, its last act would
also take place in Jerusalem. Only the center was important: the periphery was dark and badly lit. Furthermore,
what took place at the center would naturally have
consequences for the periphery. Thus, one could remain
at the center, in Jerusalem. That is where the Temple
was and the apostles. The Christ would return there.[20]

Or, in the words of J.-J. von Allmen: "If the mission of the
New Testament seems at first to be centrifugal, it is in order to
be centripetal. One goes into the world to gather, one throws
a net in order to bring it in, one sows in order to harvest."[21] In
going to seek for the nations where they are and in bringing
them to Jerusalem, the evangelization of the pagans brings the
Scriptures to their *pleroma*. The mission, therefore, is forever
"second" in relationship to a "first" which is constant: the covenant of God, the indefectible marriage of God with a particular
people. "If Israel were not, the world would not have sub-
sisted."[22]

This is valid for eternity. Jesus who became "Christ" incarnates the marriage between God and his People. He brings this
marriage to its ultimate goal, life for the whole world. In him,
with him, the bride Israel "saved herself by becoming a
mother" (cf. Tim. 2:15) of all nations. "All is accomplished."

6. | Paul and the Law

What was in need of being accomplished in Israel was the Torah (Law). No other context could be more immediate to a Jewish mind than this one when hearing the Crucified cry "all is fulfilled." That is why in the early Church, and ever since, the actual import of such an accomplishment of the Law by the Nazarene had to be assessed. This indeed is the central issue for Christianity of all times. It is expressed in several fashions, all ending up at the fundamental question: how is the cross on Calvary the decisive obedience to God's word? How does it start an entirely new era?

Jesus was hailed by the early Church as the Messiah of Israel precisely because they saw in his career and in his very life and death the fulfillment of the Holy Scriptures. Their conviction stands or falls on that issue. So the Pharisee from Tarsus, who became the apostle *par excellence,* claimed to have "seen the light" on the way to Damascus when he realized that the Nazarene he was persecuting (in the persons of Jesus' followers) was indeed the accomplishment of Israel's expectation. Paul saw the whole of his task in the assessment of the bearing of the messiahship of the Nazarene upon the nature of Torah. Jesus is the Christ because he fulfills the Torah. The economy of the accomplished Torah has now started. What is the nature of this new era?

Without Paul and his radical interpretation of Jesus' person and message, Christianity would have remained a Jewish party. The Judeo-Christian sect of the Ebionites proves this. It even suggests that Christianity without Paul would have died a few years after its inception. But Paul's attitude towards the Law was very early seen as expressing a so-called "antinomianism" totally unacceptable to Israel, thus making Christianity a new religion and breaking its bonds with Judaism.

Early in New Testament times, Paul was accused of speaking against the Law (Acts 18:13; 21:28; 25:8) and of teaching "all the Jews in the non-Jewish world to give up Moses." (Acts 21:21, my translation) His enemies in Corinth accused him of tampering with God's word (2 Cor. 4:2) and of proclaiming a different Jesus, another gospel. They said that he was inspired by an alien spirit. He appeared to derive his commission from his own authority (2 Cor. 3:5) and not from the agelong tradition of his fathers. In the Judeo-Christian documents of the Pseudo-Clementine literature (second century) we read: "How can he [Jesus] have appeared to you [Paul] when you believe the exact opposite of his doctrine?"[1] "Peter" continues by denouncing Paul's twisting of the truth. "By many expositions Paul aimed at the dissolution of the Law."[2] He is "a-nomos";[3] in fact he is the Antichrist.[4] The same argument is mentioned, to be refuted, by James and the elders when they welcome Paul and congratulate him on his apostolate among the Gentiles: " 'Jews . . . have been told about you that you teach all the Jews who are among the Gentiles to forsake Moses. . . . [But] . . . all will know that there is nothing in what they have been told about you but that you yourself live in observance of the law.' " (Acts 21:20–21, 24)

According to Travers Herford and H. J. Schonfield, it may even be that Paul is referred to in such rabbinic texts as *Sanhedrin* 107b and *Sota* 47a under the name of Gehazi, leading others into sin and incapable of repentance.[5]

Paul has thus always been a controversial figure. His dialectical thinking has never been easy to comprehend. Peter says: "our beloved brother Paul wrote to you according to the wisdom given him. . . . There are some things in . . . [his letters] hard to understand." (2 Pet. 3:15–16) Peter may have had in mind any number of things in Paul's letters, but the overall drift of the documents, testifying as they do to the historical clash between the two men, suggests that what he's referring to here is precisely Paul's interpretation of the Law (cf. Gal. 2:11ff.). The assurance of Paul, his lack of equivocation in expressing himself about such a difficult subject, could be easily construed as a lack of necessary nuances. No wonder his readers felt uncomfortable with the apostle's insistence on his revolutionary view and his impassioned arguments. As if to add to the difficulty of understanding his conception, none of his statements could be isolated as a summary of the rest of his "doctrine." The very complexity of his teaching yielded the expected outcome that there were almost as many "Pauls" as readers of Paul!

Today, even after nearly twenty centuries of Pauline studies, any hope of retrieving the apostle's genuine thought must be given up. Too much alluvial sediment has accumulated over the original riverbed, and too much time has elapsed between the epistles' *Sitz im Leben* and ours. This latter argument is especially decisive. Even if we succeeded in rediscovering the "genuine" Paul, the result of our research would have a merely antiquarian interest. For Paul spoke and wrote specifically for his contemporaries, meeting them in the very midst of their particular conditions. He addressed himself to their circumstantial problems—and with these our modern concerns have little or nothing to do. In other words, Saul of Tarsus would assuredly write today in an entirely different way about the same or different topics. To appeal to the apostle's sayings in order to justify any modern dogmatic stand is missing the point. Paul's "doctrine" is no timeless and spaceless philosophy.

One of the most grievous twists of Saul's thinking has been to "canonize" his correspondence. For his writings are situational letters. As Edgar J. Goodspeed rightly said, to Paul and his readers the epistles were *parerga,* and there was no pressing motive for their preservation.[6] Moreover they were issued separately, and therefore could not have had the massive impact they do as a collection. True, it might be tempting to pass the same judgment on the books of the Bible in general. One major difference, however, must be underlined: the Pauline letters have not become the property of a historical people ceaselessly reshaping its Scriptures to make them the perfect expression of the confirmation provided by its ongoing experience; they are the work of one man, not the product of collective reflection. Once again, they are *letters;* had he known in advance the destiny of his "casual" writings, Paul no doubt either would have written differently or perhaps written nothing at all. His style in the epistles is abrupt, nervous, impatient, passionate, polemical; sentences are left unfinished; expressions are unfortunate; the author gives a general impression of antinomianism which is misleading.[7]

Given these circumstances, is there still any justification and validity in writing a chapter of this book on "Paul and the Law"? Don't these premises condemn in advance any attempt to treat this topic? Yes and no. Yes, if our purpose were a historical reconstruction of Paul. No, if on the basis of what I have said we try to understand the *motivation* of the Jew of Tarsus. Even so, however, the endeavor is a difficult one. As in the case of Jesus of Nazareth or of the Baal Shem Tov, the traditional sayings which would sustain critical scrutiny as to their authenticity are scarce. The inescapable conclusion is that the *spirit* of those giants is expressed both *in* and *in spite of* their recorded and edited "logia." That spirit, however, is incredibly alive and forceful. It has been capable of inspiring innumerable people. Somehow, such a spirit is pressing and demanding. It is difficult to remain indifferent. One must commit oneself and communicate with the message. Such a phenomenological approach is grounded on historical and textual criticism, but it goes much further than this merely preparatory laying of foundations. The aim is to dialogue with Paul; the point is to understand what moved him to say what he said. This, I claim, is the only thing still within our reach, but, at least, it *is* something we can actually do.

Paul's pessimism regarding the Law's fulfillment by Israel runs parallel to his castigation of human corruption in general. Paul's conception of the Law is intimately dependent on his anthropology. Of course, it is out of the question to study this point at any length here, but as no real understanding of the problem discussed in this chapter can dispense with an incursion into Paul's *Menschanschauung,* I shall recall briefly some of its basic tenets.

Humanity has not been created as a final product. Human beings are, as we have seen earlier in this book, a "gerundive," something in need of completion. Originally, they are "animate beings" (cf. Gen. 2:7); ultimately, they must become "life-giving spirits" (cf. 1 Cor. 15:45). In other words, before people are transfigured into their authentic selves, they remain unachieved, unrealized, imperfect. This is what Paul means when he speaks of the "flesh." Not that there is any dualism between flesh/body and soul, but we are wholly flesh (*sarkikos* in Paul's vocabulary) as long as we are willing to "corrupt our ways" (cf. Gen. 6:11). "All flesh" means all humanity because all have chosen evil against good, death against life.

Being "flesh" is therefore a state of mind, a willfulness which denies God (cf. 1 Cor. 1:21; 2:12; 3:19).[8]

Such "carnal" humanity must necessarily die, since it has gone astray from the divine source of life. We are not mortal, but our choice is deadly; the world is not chaotic, carrying its own destruction within itself, but it goes towards its annihilation "not by its own choice, but because of him who made it so." (Rom. 8:20, my translation) We are thus rent between our own creaturely identity with the image of God, and a suicidal choice of alienation, a desire for death (Rom. 6:21) which resembles the Freudian "death instinct" *(thanatos).* Appropriately, Paul calls this aspect "the old Adam," i. e., the one in us who already has one foot in the grave, the one who flees far from the "tree" of life.

The Torah comes at this point and reveals our true selves to us. Torah is life in the midst of death, light in the midst of darkness, living water in the midst of the desert (cf. Deut. 30:15, 19; 32:47; Ps. 1:3; Isa. 55:1ff.; Rev. 7:17). Torah is not mystical. It is not esoteric or elitist. It is not reserved for some selected philosophers, or for an aristocracy of the spirit. Torah is for all, i. e., for beings of flesh and blood, of history and geography, of

politics and economy. Torah is for a social body without dis-
crimination or restriction, without *numerus clausus* or weigh-
ing of virtues. This definite exotericism of Torah guarantees its
universalism. Torah " 'is not too hard for you, neither is it far off.
It is not in heaven, that you should say "Who will go up for us
to heaven, and bring it to us, that we may hear it and do it?"
... But the word is very near you; it is in your mouth and in your
heart, so that you can do it' "[9] (Deut. 30:11–12, 14; cf. the Chris-
tological application of this text by Paul in Rom. 10:6–8); John
echoes this idea in stating that "the true light . . . enlightens
every man." (John 1:9)

Thus, Torah is made for people, and especially for those who
receive it as their light and their life. Torah is indeed inseparable from the people for whom it is meant. The two are truly one.
In parallel to the declaration that Torah is light enlightening
every man, it is striking to realize that Israel is also called the
"light to the nations." (Isa. 42:6; 49:6) In fact, any quality belonging to Torah is applicable to Israel, for Israel's vocation is
precisely to become the incarnate Torah. One could say that
Israel, as the light to the nations, has received but one commandment—to become the model of authenticity for all.

Paul, to be sure, has no quarrel with Torah as such. Not only
would it be unthinkable coming from a Jew, but it is indeed the
very opposite of his message (cf. Rom. 7:7, 13ff., etc.). But, in the
language of Paul, Torah has become, on the basis of the Greek
translation in the Septuagint, *"nomos."* Now it is well known
that Torah does not mean *nomos,* law, but instruction, orienta-
tion, way of life. This shift in the vocabulary is therefore
far-reaching. For it betrays a basic understanding (or misunderstanding) of Torah in Hellenistic Judaism. *Paul's criticism is
directly aimed at that interpretation.* He constantly refers to
the Torah *under its aspect of nomos.* This point is substantiated
by the fact that statements are expressed about *"nomos"* which
would be impossible for a Jew to maintain as such about Torah
(see, e. g., Rom. 2:23; 3:21; 4:15; 5:20; 7:4, etc.).[10]

This semantic evolution of the meaning of Torah is to be
traced back at least to the time of Ezra-Nehemiah. The Jewish

community of the restoration saw itself in danger of actual
extinction through assimilation by the nations. So few people
had come back to Zion from exile and the foreign presence was
so overwhelming that Israel's leaders reacted in a drastic way.
According to tradition they "built a fence around the Torah"
(cf. *Pirkē Aboth* 1:1: *"siyag la-Torah"*). This literally saved Judaism, but it also caused the people to withdraw into themselves
and to live *on* the Torah. Subtly but actually, Torah became
exteriorized, a code, a legal constitution of the nation, an initiation preliminary to one's membership in God's people.[11] This
was twisting the meaning of the covenant. For the Torah had
been granted to an existing people whose faith had for centuries[12] been "reckoned . . . as righteousness." (Gen. 15:6; cf.
Paul's repeated reference to this text in Rom. 4:3, 9, 22; Gal. 3:6)
For, in the beginning was God's love which constituted a people
of his own. Later, as a free gift, yes, as a bride granted by her
father to the groom, Torah was given to them.

For Paul, this chronological sequence is important, for it
emphasizes the error of believing, as a certain form of Judaism
does, that the Torah is a condition to fulfill in order to be God's
people. The love of God is in fact unconditional (Rom. 3:23;
4:16; 5:17, 20, etc.). "Gospel" comes before the "Law" (cf. Gal.
3:7–18; Rom. 4:9–18), as Karl Barth has insisted. If it were not
so, nobody would be in a position to be loved.

Nonetheless, Torah had become a Law. From being an end,
it had become a means; from being life, it had become a way
of life. The fence erected around the Torah secluded Israel
from the rest of humanity, in violation of the nature of election
which—as we have seen above—is not exclusive but inclusive.
In other words, Judaism became a kind of pietism, and like all
other pietisms of history it substituted itself for the world and
became in itself a complete, full-fledged universe, the only valid
reality, relegating all the rest to nonbeing.

Once again an inexorable "law" was verified in the be-
liever's life: the more something is holy and "divine" the more
easily it becomes a stumbling block. Sacrifices are holy, but
when they allow for the stiffening of the neck with good con-

science, they are an instrument of sin. In Hosea 6:6, for example, "mercy" and "sacrifices" are not two principles set in opposition. The point is that mercy includes sacrifices, but sacrifices can be offered without mercy, and then they are a parody of holiness (cf. Luke 11:42). Life is shortchanged into technique when the focus is shifted from God's grace to our own performance.

Paul took over the prophetic protest that Torah becomes an escape when it is used as an instrument to secure happiness and prosperity, blessings and protection, when it becomes a means for being singled out by God and saved. God has nothing to do with the "bourgeois" of the spirit. Dietrich Bonhoeffer tears such notions apart when he says: "When Christ calls a man, he bids him come and die."[13]

As indicated above, it is mainly in reference to such a distortion of the Torah's essence that Paul uses the term *"nomos."* Paul states that the Law has proved to be ambivalent: as protection of Israel's authenticity, it has also become a wall of separation from the nations and has thus prevented Israel from fulfilling her vocation as light to the Gentiles.

This shortcoming had the gravest consequences, not only for the nations, but in the first place for Israel. For her aim was diverted in the process: instead of bringing Torah to fulfillment for the sake of the world's redemption, the Law became an occasion for some to "ignore God's way of righteousness, and to try to set up their own. . . . For the Anointed is the *telos* of the Law and he brings righteousness for *everyone* who has faith." (Rom. 10:3–4, my translation)

Paul became "the apostle to the nations" with the consciousness of filling an essential gap in his people's vocation. True, Israel's accomplishment of "the law of commandments and ordinances" (Eph. 2:15) does *ipso facto* benefit the whole world. But the "groanings of the whole created universe in all its parts as if in the pangs of childbirth" (Rom. 8:22, my translation) are hardly audible to the saints when their primary concern is for their own salvation and commerce with God. The terrible mistake of some in Israel—the deadliness of which Jesus and Paul were fully aware—is to have reduced Torah to the level of a "religion." The Jews are actually the true (dynamic) image of humanity, or else they become self-complacent and, eventually, totally "useless" for the world's sake. Torah then becomes a code of justice, a chart of ethics, a *vade mecum* of the perfect Pharisee. Then the Jews make the Torah, not the Torah the Jews. God's word is no longer life but a recipe for an honest behavior (cf. Gal. 3:21).

Against such an "automation" of Israel's existence, Paul recalls that "justice . . . is no external legality, imputed by observance of the Law or by God's decree. It is something imprinted in man's being, involving his entire renewal."[14] *Paul calls faith the internalization of Torah,* to which he opposes what he calls "the law of works." (Rom. 3:27, my translation) To be sure, the internalized Torah produces "works"; there is no life without manifestations of life (cf. the book of James). But life is not the mere accumulation of its manifestations. Life goes infinitely beyond existence; love is infinitely greater than lovemaking; our true selves go infinitely beyond our physical deeds. Thus, when Pastor Dietrich Bonhoeffer decided with his uncle and friends to assassinate Hitler, in flagrant opposition to the commandment not to commit murder, he in fact fulfilled the Torah. And, before him, Moses and Ehud, Jael and Judith, in strict legalism murderers, accomplished God's design, for the Torah is not a code. Similarly, to use contraceptives today *may* be, despite Genesis 1:28, the fulfillment of Torah. In the crucible of life, disobedience is more often than not the true obedience. There is no need for any kind of casuistry to justify this.

Inescapably, we must use the Pauline categories of "spirit" and "letter" (cf. 2 Cor. 3:6, "the letter kills, but the spirit gives life" [my translation]), although not in order to create a false dichotomy between the one and the other. The spirit is conveyed by the letter. But the spirit transcends the letter as much as our "soul" transcends our physical components. No one more than the Jew knows how much people must be considered, not according to " 'the outward appearance, . . . [for] the LORD looks on the heart.' " (1 Sam. 16:7) True, as far as Torah is concerned the outward appearance is not deceitful. But the "works of law" (Rom. 3:28) can be. That is why Paul exclaims in the same verse: "we hold that a man is justified by faith apart from works of law."

It is thus legitimate at this point to revise the judgment of antinomianism leveled against Paul. He himself claims to be a lover of Torah.[15] "Do we then overthrow the law by this faith? By no means! On the contrary, we uphold the law." (Rom. 3:31) For Torah, in his eyes, is not *a* way of life, it *is* life. In fact, it is embodied in the person of the Central Jew.

This crucial affirmation not only by Paul but by the primitive Church as a whole is clearly grounded on a conception of Torah which we have once more to appraise. For Paul and his followers, Torah is dynamic, it is the life of the authentic Israel, i. e., the history both lived and to be lived by those who *choose* to find their identity in that divine revelation (cf. Ps. 37:31; Isa. 51:7). Torah is therefore not the best possible moral code, but the ongoing history of the relationship with God. For Paul, this means the history of the Anointed who is the head of the corporate body.

Now history is the opposite of a blueprinted pattern. To "go by the rule" as if history were a game is perhaps safe, but it always converts life into a technique. Hence the severity of Paul in denouncing such a corruption of Torah (cf. Gal. 2:7–9, 12; Rom. 2:25–26; 3:1, 30, etc.). To go by the rule is to show no respect for the Torah; it kills the Torah and sterilizes its promise. Torah then becomes "Law" and even so an inoperative, impotent one. To call this protest of Paul's antinomianism is a grave misunderstanding. Moses himself would agree that when the contract is substituted for relationship, it is better to have no contract at all. Torah is great, but still greater is what Torah advocates: the relationship of people to God.

I have shown in earlier chapters that suffering and self-sacrifice are coextensive with Israel's vocation. All other responses to God's demand are the fruits of hybris. For all other responses necessarily have *self* as their ultimate goal; God is evacuated or, worse, he is used for our satisfaction. All other responses are *religious,* i. e., they are the most refined means ever invented to appease our conscience while exploiting the greatest possible power: the power of the gods. What distinguishes Israel from all other nations (i. e., from all other choices) is her self-renouncement. This is the opposite of religion. I mean that Israel's life is not a system, or a theory about existence, or the subtle flattering of the human will for power. Of course, Israel *kata sarka* is perfectly able to pervert her life's choice into a doctrine, a system, a religion. But then a Jesus or a Paul, like the prophets, will denounce the hoax.

It is Paul's conviction that the Torah is accomplished when the relationship of "I and Thou" is so intimate that both become an "androgynous" flesh. Then the communion is perfect; there is no hiatus between God and Israel. Then any command to love God and the neighbor becomes not only superfluous, but even offensive, since such an imperative belongs to a preliminary status of no-love before the communion between I and Thou. That is why Paul dares to say that the Law was adapted to the flesh (Gal. 3:3; 2:19; Rom. 7:6; cf. Matt. 19:8), which is another way of saying that the Law has been adapted to the nonfulfillment era, *before* the marriage of God and his people under the leadership of the Anointed.

Paul's demonstration is impressive. The Law, he says, is good (Rom. 7:16), holy, divine, blameless, spiritual (Rom. 7:14). But people are carnal (Rom. 7:14; 8:7–9), and the spiritual can only clash with what is fleshly, "sold under [that is, the slave of] sin." (Rom. 7:14) The unexpected effect of the Law is then to exacerbate human sin (Rom. 7:13) and to make sin which was previously "not counted" into a transgression (Rom. 5:13). Thus the Law brings within itself its own contradiction: meant to spiritualize and liberate (Rom. 7:10, 14, 15, 17, 18, etc.), it instead multiplies the noxiousness of sin. For we all discover another law, namely the "law of the limbs" (Rom. 7:23, my translation) which forces us to alienate ourselves, against our will (7:15, 19, 20, 21).[16]

God inaugurates the new era by resolving the contradiction of the Law in a living person. Torah "came to dwell among us," more accurately it came to "tabernacle" (John 1:14, my translation), in the person of the Central Jew. His fulfillment of the Torah is in becoming Torah. In him, human beings and their choice are "sealed together." The carnal is consumed in the spiritual; the flesh leaves all the room to the spirit. The Nazarene makes it true in actually consuming the whole of his life in a total offering, *le-šem ha-šamayim,* for the love of God. But, behold, when the "last of the just" is dead, he miraculously "sees his offspring, he prolongs his days." (Isa. 53:10, my translation) Instead of the expected emptiness of all meaning in his life, an innumerable crowd throughout centuries witnesses the emptiness of his tomb. After the extermination of the Jews, after the strangulation of innocence, Hitler thought that only nothingness remained; whereas the whole horizon was filled with God.

To acknowledge this is the most unwarranted move ever. To affirm victory in failure, life-finding in life-losing, life in death, is the most illogical, the most irrational, the most "irreligious" cry of sanity in the midst of insanity. But it is also the greatest revolutionary act of all, for it not only liberates us from any performance principle, but even from ourselves. There is no longer anything for us to achieve, there is nothing to prove.[17] Life is not a calculation of successes, of virtues, of good deeds. We only find life when we surrender our whole self to God so that God "fills all in all."

Without our participation then, and eventually without us altogether? Not at all. Humanity is the necessary herald of God's victory. Earlier in this book, I called attention to the fact that without our human expression of God's creating act, *be-r'ešit bara Elohim,* God's creation misses its object. Here similarly, it is our human *faith* which empties Christ's tomb.

In the words of the Baal Shem Tov " 'Everybody in Israel has to restore and to prepare that part of the structure of the Messiah *(komat mashiah)* which belongs to his own soul . . . until the whole structure will be restored and established and then there will be a permanent and universal *yihud,* realization of unity.' "[18] The point of departure is thus the same as for Paul. The messianic fulfillment is—really for Paul, virtually for Hasidism—behind us. We live in an "already/not yet" tension whose "impossibility" is tolerable only in faith.

For the whole question is to know what kind of event is capable of swinging the promise into fulfillment, and to make present the future of "you shall be my people and I shall be your God." Now, if we follow Jeremiah (cf. 31:31ff.), that event is clearly the coming of a time when people actually participate in the spirit of the Torah: Torah will be written "upon their hearts." But if so, the point is not for Israel to exhaust herself in fulfilling the 613 commandments and prohibitions of the Torah transformed into Law, but rather to become herself the living Torah (cf. Rom. 10:8). In the latter case, the 613 commandments are but 613 aspects of one reality which transcends them all. 613,000 other aspects could be added without ever reaching more than an approximation of the living being called Torah.

Paul is overwhelmed by the cross in which he sees the very soul of Torah. For, if Torah is the record of authentic relationship with God, it then bears testimony to the one who by love gave up his life on the gallows. In acknowledging this, Paul views the accomplishment as total, while the promise is not exhausted in a post-historical status quo. The promise remains promise; to love succeeds love.

In the person of the Nazarene is revealed the impossibility of fulfilling the Torah *and* continuing to live. For "if Christ is in you, your bodies, it is true, are for death because of sin." (Rom. 8:10, my translation) Just as it was impossible for life and sin to coexist (Rom. 5:12, 21; 6:23), so also no one can live and attempt as well to satisfy the Absolute. Only God can satisfy God. He did so in graciously accepting the supreme sacrifice of his "Son" whom he "raised from the dead." (Rom. 10:7, my translation) " 'Man shall not see me and live,' " says God (Exod. 33:20). Conversely, no one shall see God without dying. Death "in a kiss of the Lord" as Deuteronomy 34:5 says, according to the rabbis, consumes our human no-love, it consumes our incapacity for the absolute, our no-life!

After Auschwitz, it may seem offensive to equate Israel's fulfillment with death. For Emil Fackenheim, the Jews today have received the commandment to survive, for their death would be granting a posthumous victory to Hitler the slaughterer. However, survival cannot be divorced from what constitutes the very *raison d'être* of Israel. There is a prolongation of existence which also gives to Hitler a posthumous victory. To survive at the cost of one's identity is also to lose the battle. The "Capos" in the concentration camps did survive! The Jews have received the commandment to live *as Jews*. Precisely at this point the argumentation of Paul finds its insertion. For him, the alternatives are not to exist or to perish. The opposite of the Jews' survival is not death, but infidelity, apostasy, sin; in modern language, alienation, despair, nihilism. In the greatest paradox ever, Paul, following Jesus, proclaims the supreme sacrifice *le-qidduš ha-šem* (for the sanctification of the Name) as survival; he proclaims death (that kind of death which has nothing to do with Hitler's annihilation) as fulfillment of one's integrity. If bare Jewish survival were the way to deprive Hitler of his victory, the "man of nothingness" would have been victorious 6 million times. But the prophetic message of the author of the Servant Songs, of Jesus of Nazareth, of Paul, of Rabbi Akiba, of Israel, is that Hitler has been 6 million times defeated by his victims. The latter did in fact survive as witnesses of the triumph of true humanity, yes even of the triumph of God. "God raised them up, having loosed the pangs of death, because it was not possible for them to be held by it" (cf. Acts 2:24).

Appendix A to Chapter 6
Reflections on Faith as
Internalization of Torah According to
Paul

The process of internalization of Torah in early Christianity is as much the product of the time-*Geist* as a display of genius. It corresponds to both an actual necessity from a pragmatic point of view, and a long-range vision much in advance of its generation.

I intend here to draw a parallel between the aforementioned process and a comparable and concomitant evolution of another literary genre, the narrative. This latter category is singled out here because it offers a privileged term of comparison. It is so, first, because the literary genre of narrative is much less invested with theological passion than is Law in both Judaism and Christianity. Moreover, the very mechanism of internalization (one could say "psychologization") is infinitely more patent and easier to understand in the narrative than in the realm of the "philosophy of the Law."

The narrative in Hebrew Scriptures, especially in its comparatively early form, is characterized by its art of understatement or litote. According to the definition given to it by Scholes and Kellogg, the litote is the "ironic tension between the cool narrative tone and the violence which the reader imagines within the minds of the characters."[19] One thinks for example of the "binding of Isaac" in Genesis 22. The text could not be any more sober than it is. Not a single word is superfluous. There is no distraction from the inexorable external progression of the events. At no point are we told about the turmoil in the souls of the protagonists. Nevertheless, we are made conscious of an extraordinary emotional power unexpressed but all the more present in the narrative. A succession of precisions such as we find in verse 2 brings the text to the extreme limit of the litote and is charged with an intensity of feeling that the greatest Romantics hardly reach. "He said: 'Take your son, your only son Isaac, whom you love . . . .' "

Most remarkable, however, is the fact that the use of understatement and the age of a literary piece are in direct proportion. A comparison between the "sagas" of the patriarchs in the book of Genesis, on the one hand, and the later and more complicated Joseph novel, on the other, is revealing. In the latter, we find descriptions such as this: "Then Joseph could not control himself before all those who stood by

him, and he cried." (Gen. 45:1) Or, in the same vein, in Genesis 46:29,
"Joseph . . . presented himself to him [his father], and fell on his neck,
and wept on his neck a good while." Scholes and Kellogg recall the
litote about David sinning with Bathsheba (2 Sam. 11) and, on the other
hand, Jesus' declaration about adultery as soon as a man *looks* at a
woman with lust.[20] Regarding this last example, it should be noted that
with the advent of Hellenism in the fourth century B.C.E., the need was
felt of the passage from the outward to the inward. The "landslide"
triumph of individualism could not content itself any longer with so
much restraint in expressing one's feelings. The times were ripe for the
unabashed display of sentiments, inner struggles, personal efforts of
adaptation to the esthetic or moral canons of society. The arts, by the
way, suffered from such narcissism, but that is not our concern here.
Whether by fashion or incapacity, people were no longer moved by
external expressions of the soul. These were (wrongly) equated with an
absence of emotion. If bed pillows were not described as soaked with
the hero's tears, you had to conclude that he was a brute and a rogue.
No "spontaneous" act of generosity could occur without being introduced and followed by rhetorical displays of *"grandeur d'âme."*

When we pass from the narrative to the legislative realm, it is clear
that mere obedience to the laws without some discourse on their effect
on the soul was construed rightly or wrongly as mere legalism. The
"Law" was in need of being reinterpreted from the point of view of
the "inward" lest it become purely formal and deprived of its *original*
and *intended* "spirit." True, as we have seen, emotion was far from
absent in the older culture, and the Torah had never been intended
as a cold code of laws. When the new culture arose, however, the lack
of emotional expression was felt as a sterilizing absence, and one must
say that a certain attachment to "the letter of the Law"—pale remain-
der of the epoch of the understatement—did give some validity to
what was primarily a misunderstanding by the newer sensitivity.
Hence the necessity of "reformers" such as Jesus, Paul, or the Baal
Shem Tov, for making explicit and unmistakable the substance of
Torah. They do not propose another Torah, nor certainly the cancella-
tion of Torah. They only want to give Torah back its rationale and its
project. As George Steiner says (about "translation"), "The letter
changes; the spirit is intact yet made new."[21]

Appendix B to Chapter 6
A Preface to the Dialogue:
Reassessing the Nature of the New
Testament

In the discussion above in this chapter, I have said that Paul's letters were *"parerga,"* circumstantial writings which neither their author nor their first recipients expected would become "canonical." I then indicated that such writings cannot be put on the same plane with those found in the Hebrew Scriptures. This issue is clearly of utmost importance. The authority of the "New Testament" is at stake and, for many Christians, it is a "taboo" topic, blasphemous even to consider. That is, however, what I intend to do in this appendix, for several reasons. The least important one is that the notion of "taboos" has no home in Judeo-Christianity. Even if "not all things are necessarily helpful," nevertheless "all *are* permitted." (1 Cor. 6:12, my translation) Moreover, a misconception of the "New Testament" has constituted a roadblock in the dialogue between Jews and Christians; the Christian "Bible" does not conform with the Jewish one! Therefore, however far one is ready to go and meet those of the other faith, there is a point which cannot be trespassed and where the two part. Soon enough the time comes when the Christian partners take refuge behind the un-touchability of their own "Scriptures" and thus make the dialogue impossible.[22] This, I just said, is done from a vantage point which is a misunderstanding of the nature of the New Testament. And this is the third and main reason for my endeavor here.

It is essential that one realize that the Hebrew Scriptures are the record of Israel's history grounded in her conjugal relationship with God. The Bible's matter and *telos* is the *"Heilsgeschichte."* It pro-claims the message of the People's "plus-being" and, as such, reflects the whole of Israel's soul in its psychological and historical dimen-sions. Thus, inasmuch as they are words of those who live the very history of God, Scriptures have, understandably, another characteris-tic, namely, contradiction. Anthropology for God rather than theol-ogy for man, as Abraham Heschel said, those existential documents do not shrink from putting the Yes and the No under the wing of the transcending One. Such an achievement demands both the flashing intuition of the presence of eternity in the moment, and the long-suffering patience before the fragmentation of the message throughout the endless duration of history "from alpha to omega."

And indeed Israel's Scriptures were composed during numerous centuries, first in their oral form, then throughout the slow process of their literary development. A considerable span of time was necessary for the individual Jew or the priestly and prophetic People to successively internalize the presence of the Deuteronomist and of Job. Still more time was necessary to feed on them simultaneously. In fact, there is no end to this painful parturition. The canon of Scriptures does not mark the end of the process. With it, the history of traditions does not come to a stop. The canon merely acknowledges a written compendium as representing, effectively although minimally, all aspects of Israel's soul. But as for the living tradition, i. e., the dialogue of the People with history, it is not thereby exhausted. It expresses itself with a remarkable vigor in the Pesharim, Talmudim, Midrashim, Responsa, Kabbala, etc.

There is a place, therefore, *beside* the Scriptures, but without confusing the two, for the expression of an "oral" tradition. As such its only *raison d'être* is to refer to the Scriptures, and to shed upon them a new/old light. The canon is constituted in its "untouchability," but the oral tradition is the existential acknowledgment of the open-endedness of Scriptures in the image of the unendedness of the *Heilsgeschichte*. The tradition does not take the place of Scriptures, and it does not even "complete" them, but it explains, explicates, and actualizes them. It prevents Scriptures from becoming for their readers a dead letter. The oral tradition is the *reading* of the "letter"; as such it is life-giving.

From that perspective, the "New Testament" is "one" Jewish reading of the Scriptures among others. It is so, not only because it is written by Jews about the Central Jew, but also because of its "conjugal" relation with the Hebrew canon. The New Testament is a collection of Midrashim, i. e., one legitimate reading of the Scriptures.[23] That it opposes other Jewish traditions falls in line with, for example, the many quarrels of schools one finds on every page of the Talmud, or, for that matter the perennial confrontation between Jewish sects. Those deep differences inside Judaism did not result in divorces because it has always been acknowledged that there are "seventy" interpretations of any Biblical saying. The limit, however, is flagrantly transgressed when one tradition raises itself to the rank of the very authority which it formerly recognized as unique and which it contributed to establishing, i. e., the Holy Scriptures.

The earliest writer to mention part of the New Testament (Paul's letters) as *graphē* (Scripture), is the author of 2 Peter (3:15–16).[24] This runs counter to the rest of New Testament literature. There, the numerous references to *graphē* or *graphai* are uniformly to the Hebrew Bible. Acts 17:11 summarizes this general situation; it reads (my translation): "These Jews of Beroea received the message eagerly, studying the Scriptures each day to see whether it was as Paul and Silas said." All other uses of *graphē* in the New Testament testify to the eagerness of the writers to found their message not upon their own authority but unequivocally upon "the Torah and the Prophets." It may very well be that in bringing their testimony about the coincidence they saw between the written and the lived, they themselves uttered prophetic words. But our problem lies somewhere else. The Talmud tells us that once Moses himself was overwhelmed, and somewhat humiliated, by the teaching of Rabbi Akiba exposing "the Torah of Moses."[25] This provided no grounds for the Synagogue to consider Rabbi Akiba's teaching as canonical!

The history of the "New Testament" canonization extends through several centuries. Some of its books began to be regarded as Holy Scripture by the end of the second century. Others saw their authority disputed for three or four hundred years. Moreover, the category of "holy" books was somewhat fluid. There was no clearcut borderline separating profane from sacred writings. The presence of numerous so-called apocryphal Gospels proves the fact. The latter were put in that category only when four among them were canonized. As F. W. Beare puts it: "when the gospels came to be written and passed gradually into general use in the churches, the authority they acquired was accorded to them, not in the first instance as holy books, but as books containing the holy words of Jesus. The authority of the words was primary; that of the books was secondary and derivative." The same author rightly states: "The earliest Christian writings . . . were occasional writings, addressed by the apostle to particular churches . . . [and] not intended for general circulation in the church . . . let alone [to be] treasured by the whole church and given a place alongside the Law and the Prophets in worship and in study."[26] We can therefore broaden Edgar J. Goodspeed's judgment about Paul's letters and include all of the New Testament works: they were *parerga*.[27] Also the Gospels are, to a certain extent, letters. Their nature is not essentially different from the circumstantial, contextual, even casual epistles of the apostle Paul.

One cannot overlook the fact that the time of the New Testament canon's formation coincides with the Christian onslaught against Judaism and the hardening of the Church's dogmatism. Unlike the canonization by the rabbis in Yamnia (Jabne) of the so-called "Old Testament," the exaltation of Christian writings to the level of "holy scriptures" is to a noticeable extent "anti" something, namely anti-Jewish and eventually anti-Semitic. It is no small paradox that Jewish writings were thus used as tools for anti-Jewish propaganda. This was made possible through a systematic devaluation of Hebrew Scriptures and the corresponding mythologization of the Gospels. The more the holy character of Christian texts was emphasized, the more de-Judaized they appeared to their readers. The Word lost all of its flesh, despite John 1:14, and the idealized "Jesus" became the founder of a new religion grounded upon its own scriptures.[28] To add insult to injury, and in an "Oedipal" move of revolt against the Jewish "father," the Hebrew tradition was also claimed as more or less authoritative; it was stolen from the Jews.[29]

This situation was unavoidable. The coexistence of two canons is an inner contradiction. By definition, a canon is fundamentally altered by any addition or subtraction. A canon is forever sufficient; it is as brief and complete, as precise and reliable, as a geometrical theorem. It stands or falls within those precise limits. True, the Hebrew Scriptures are accompanied, as we have seen, by an "oral" tradition. It is in that spirit that the Gospels were initially conceived. But when a tradition is translated from the periphery to the center it unavoidably displaces the former center to the periphery.

As the theory goes in the Church, the two canons have become one with two parts: an "old" testament and a "new" testament. Practically, however, the marriage has proven unsuccessful. The very names "Old Testament" and "New Testament" used to describe the two partners show that an order of priorities was established between the two and that they were conceived *ab initio* as unequal. The "new" is unmistakably destined to replace the "old." Such an understanding is not due to mere naiveté. It is understood in the Church that the Old Testament is preparation to the New, for it was "merely a hint of what was to come." (Col. 2:17, my translation; cf. Heb. 8:5; 10:1) Moreover, the liturgy of many churches supposes that one listens to the "Old Testament reading" while sitting in one's place, but to the "gospel" in a standing position.

Therefore, if Christians really want to free the Church from the anti-Semitic poison, if they actually intend to stop the fateful evolution which started with Marcion and ended up with Alfred Rosenberg, they must be willing to extirpate the root of evil. Now, especially since Jules Isaac's works, we have been made aware that such a root is sadly in the New Testament itself. To eradicate it, a few elucidations will not suffice. For even before we turn to the content of the New Testament, there is a problem more urgent and more fundamental. Some scholars, for instance, disturbed by the fourth Gospel's use of anti-Jewish vocabulary, tried to sweeten its slanderous character. They identified "the

Jews" there with the priestly class of Sadducees, or the leading disreputable party of collaborators with Rome.[30] The enterprise deserves our praises, but remains superficial. The issue is not solved in flanking the texts with explanatory notes in order to soften their offensiveness. One must go much deeper than that; the solutions must be more radical. Christians must reappraise the New Testament literatures. A new respect for their nature as *"parerga"* must emerge, and a new liberty must be exerted towards them. The anti-Semitic character of their canonization must be unequivocally confessed.[31]

As a reader of the Christian kerygma, I am not bound to condone the enmity, or even the bigoted hatred of the Jews in John's or Matthew's writings. Whatever their reasons were for resorting to such below-the-belt blows, they are not excusable and they certainly cannot become a model and a guide for their readers. The inescapable conclusions of the historical criticism of the Gospels must someday be drawn. We know for a fact today that the authors' anti-Semitism led them to grave historical distortions. Such is the case for instance when they reported the events of Jesus' trial and torture. Pages like these in the "Good News" cost the lives of innumerable men, women, and children. It would be false to put all the blame for those crimes against humanity upon a misinterpretation of "innocent" texts. In fact, sheer honesty demands our acknowledgment that "the teaching of contempt" did not start with too zealous interpreters but with the documents themselves. It is true that commentators were only too happy to find this bias in the texts. The time has now come—more than a full generation after Auschwitz—to humbly confess that, were it not for the Gospels' exclusivity as carriers of the Nazarene's kerygma, they would deserve to be rejected out of hand as historically false and morally defamatory documents. But the early Gentile Church had apparently nothing better to offer.[32] Moreover, it seems a well-grounded assertion that the same Church systematically destroyed all remnants of other traditions. Such a policy of censorship leaves us with little more than take it or leave it.

Paradoxical, painful, unbearable situation for Christians! In order to encounter the Central Jew, symbol of his people for the nations, we are left no other way than to listen to the Nazarene in, and as it were *despite,* a message which falls foul of suspicion, because it has been alienated. For the tragedy—which neither the Jewish people nor the nations can ignore—is that the very message which touched the hearts of millions and brought them to Zion, despite everything else, was historically, and *therefore indispensably,* transmitted by the Gospels. Thus, without the writings of the so-called "New Testament," I am "separated from Christ, alienated from the commonwealth of Israel." (Eph. 2:12) But with them as "holy scriptures," I reject with one hand

that which I received with the other! It may be that the author of
Philippians 2 did not realize to what extremes of "emptiness" and
"servanthood" the Word had to go to be "born in the likeness of men."
But is this not also what the Midrash says about the Truth being cast
to the ground by God?[33]

To pick up the Truth's "sparks" and unite them as an offering to
God, such is the vocation of all "who are not born of flesh and of blood."
(John 1:13, my translation) Truth is always hard to listen to; it does not
flatter our instincts; it does not speak of pure or impure races; it de-
spises demagoguery and does not try to please. The Truth of the Gospels also complies with that definition. One must have the courage to
seek it inside unworthy or deceptive "barks." Yes, Truth has been cast
to the ground; but in a good soil *metanoia,* repentance, can spring up.
We are invited to return to the Temple on whose stairs the Central Jew
proclaimed a message people remember. On those very stairs the
dialogue between Jews and Christians someday shall start.

7. | The Duality
Israel-Christendom

In what precedes, I stated that the New Testament is the "oral" tradition of the Christian sect within first- and second-century Palestinian Judaism. The document's rationale is to establish its validity and credibility in its Jewish environment. That is why, as I have said, the Gospel writers were anxious to show, all along the life-itinerary of Jesus, the ongoing fulfillment of prophecies; and why Paul, in his turn, struggled with the problem of the statutes of Torah/Law in the "third" eon, the era of "all is accomplished."

We now turn to another crucial issue. The book of Acts in particular expresses well the surprising and the challenging phenomenon the Jewish early Church had to face. The "evangelion" (the "good news," Hebrew *besorah,*" cf. Isa. 40:9) was finding an amazing reception among the non-Jews of the Mediterranean countries. The event was both a bliss and a threat. Again the book of Acts reports the internal uneasiness and eventual strife it occasioned among the Christian Jews in Jerusalem. We even have a (much debilitated) narrative on the historic "council of Jerusalem" in which Paul's universalistic point of view prevailed over the more cautious approach of "Peter," i. e., the group of the Twelve (Acts 15).

Be that as it may, it is clear that the question of the relationship between Jews and non-Jews in the bosom of the Church very early became an acute problem. Furthermore, the leaders of the sect were far from unanimously gratified by the "en masse" (relatively speaking) adherence of Gentiles. History proved, by the way, that their gravest fears were not ill-founded, for soon enough the Gentile branch of the Church became so prevalent that it smothered the Jewish trunk of the Christian tree.

With the Pauline and para-Pauline epistles, however, we are not yet at that point of break. The Gentile acceptance of the gospel is still a novelty, and the theological issue it stirs is not clouded by secessionist tendencies. Paul and his followers tackle the question head on.

The author of the epistle to the Ephesians for instance is unequivocal in his affirmation of the unity of Israel and the Church. From the same perspective as that of Romans 11:17ff., which speaks of the Gentiles grafted onto the cultivated olive tree, Ephesians describes the unity of the two formerly hostile parties in terms of the Gentiles' entering into the community of "the saints and members of the household of God." (Eph. 2:19; cf. 2:12ff.) In Ephesians 2 as well as in Romans 9—11—the most explicit texts of the New Testament dealing with the problem of the new economy of relations between Jews and Gentiles —it is out of the question to consider the Church as having *replaced* the Israel of old. The household of God has become universal according to its vocation and its hope. Israel does not disappear in the process but, on the contrary, covers the world. The micro-cosmos has become the macro-cosmos. "The mountain of the Lord's house [has been] established as the top of the mountains, and [has been] exalted above the hills; and peoples flow unto it. And many nations [go] and [say]: 'Come ye, and let us go up to the mountain of the Lord, and to the house of the God of Jacob; and he will teach us of his ways, and we will walk in his paths'; for out of Zion [goes] forth the Torah, and the word of the Lord from Jerusalem." (Isa. 2:2–3=Micah 4:1–2, my translation)

But a problem internal to the New Testament literature arises: are not such stands as Romans 9—11 and Ephesians 2 contradicted by another powerful trend? What about such texts in the epistles as Romans 10:12, which proclaims (my translation) that "there is no distinction between Jews and Gentiles, the same Lord is Lord of all and bestows his riches upon all who call upon him"?[1] Does not Colossians 3:10–11 state that, after having "put on the new nature, which is being renewed in knowledge after the image of its creator . . . there cannot be Greek and Jew, circumcised and uncircumcised, barbarian, Scythian, slave, free man, but Christ is all, and in all"? Does not Galatians 3:28 proclaim much the same thing in the name of our oneness "in Christ Jesus"?[2] Granted, but these statements, conclusive though they may be, contain unexpected features and are embedded in complex contexts from which they cannot be isolated.

First of all, these three texts (Rom. 10:12; Gal. 3:28; Col. 3:10–11) concur insofar as they proclaim anew a well-known principle of the Hebrew Scriptures—God "is not partial"; " 'there is no perversion of justice with the LORD our God, or partiality, or taking bribes.' " (2 Chron. 19:7; cf. Deut. 10:17; 1 Sam. 16:7; Job 34:19)[3] This impartiality of God is focused, in the Pauline and "deutero-Pauline" epistles, on the non-distinction between Jews and Gentiles in the dispensation of God's love and concern. But other polarized realities are also reconciled when put again in God's perspective: circumcised and uncircumcised (Col.); slave and free (Gal.; Col.); barbarian, Scythian, and, by implication, civilized (Col.); male and female (Gal.). Obviously, though the lists are not exhaustive, they provide a sample of manifestly opposed poles or groups, which, being at the benefit of the same love and concern of God, are reconciled and made one. They now share this striking reality: "God fills all in all" (cf. 1 Cor. 15:28; Eph. 4:10). The primitive Church's acknowledgment that Jesus of Nazareth was in fact the King-Messiah expected by Israel, the Prime of creation expected by God, entails as a first consequence the affirmation of the unity of creation responding to the unity of God. With the Nazarene, the Shekinah (presence of the Lord) had descended again and definitively from heaven, to dwell among and in humanity. There was something new under the sun. God was saying: "Wherever traces of man's footsteps can be found, there am I."[4] A new economy had been initiated marking not the end of history but its new beginning.

In the brutal "objectivity" of the world, i. e., in its antipathetic poles, differing parties confront one another with the hate yielded by their heterogeneity. They resent each other and the incomprehensible injustice of having to face their contraries and thus in a way their own negation. Male is limited in his integrity by female; black by white; Greek by Jew; barbarian by civilized. The poles can only clash, each trying desperately to wrest the other into a conformity with itself, striving to overcome their fundamental alterity. The normal state in a polarized nature is war. There is war between the sexes, between races, between nomads and settlers, between manual laborers and intellectuals. "Countryside and town have built up two inimical realms since there has been a civilization" says Georges Sorel in his book on violence.[5] Karl Marx speaks in his turn of society as if it were cut into two fundamentally antagonistic groups, but, according to the genius he owes to his Jewishness, he overcomes the immobilism implied by his statement and boldly proclaims that "violence is the midwife of history." Here the dichotomy, which is a state of nature, must be resolved historically by the triumph of one pole over the other.

We are as a matter of fact confronting three different attitudes regarding polarized realities in the world. In an archetypical *Weltanschauung,* characterized by its static dualism, the polar values resist and deny one another, locked in an eternal, cyclical dance—as in the case of the Yin and Yang of Chinese philosophy. Wisdom consists in the difficult acceptance of the two poles as alternates. We are ultimately not responsible, for everything happens outside of us. It would be folly to engage in a history of the relationship of Yin and Yang as if we were actors in it, rather than simply "peaceful" witnesses of a process which is above our comprehension. The world is the immense tick-tock of a pendulum and we are but recorders of the ticking. Some are stirred by visionary utopias and imagine that they will change something in the relationship of sexes, races, economically distant groups; but true philosophers know these phantoms for what they are. They know that revolutions are only cosmic convulsions for bringing up a new looping of the circle. The slaves of yesterday will be the masters tomorrow, but only for a while, until the day after tomorrow when they will be slaves again. Here, there *are* "Greeks and Jews, circumcised and uncircumcised, barbarians, Scythians, slaves and free men," but their distinction causes in the absolute no problem, because the barbarian of today will be the civilized person of tomorrow. It is merely a matter of philosophy, a matter of peace of mind, a matter of passive acceptance of the inevitable.

The second stand vis-à-vis the problem is much more dynamic, but the dualism is carefully maintained. Marxism, following Hegel, envisions a transcendentalization of the rivalry between the two poles in a triumphant eschatology. The "great Evening" will come when the oppressed of the two antagonists supersedes and suppresses the oppressor forever. In the process, however, the former group will not retain its old identity, for its nature was conditioned by its subjection, whereas tomorrow it will shape reality according to its own creativity. We can therefore hardly imagine what the races or the sexes will be in such an eschatological dawning. Marxism considers "masculinity" and "femininity" culturally bound categories. They do not represent anything in particular besides the obvious physiological difference of function. When their millennia-long opposition is overcome, who knows how they will appear and what kind of world will emerge from such a profound mutation? In short, here, according to Hegelian pattern, we are invited to think in terms of a synthesis resulting from the clash between thesis (maleness) and antithesis (femaleness). In the outcome of the process, neither "Greek" nor "Jew" will ever be the same. "Greek" and "Jew" will probably appear, in that time of bliss, as relics of antiquity. Humanity will be so new and so different that the old categories will be obsolete. "Here there cannot be Greek and Jew anymore, circumcised and uncircumcised, no barbarian, no Scythian, no slave, but simply free people," i. e., a new status not exhausted by malehood and femalehood. Males and females will construct an economy fitting the new times: they will become together—and each for his/her part—human beings. The primordial dualism is resolved in a brand new third term. Hence our difficulty in completely grasping its nature. We have no precedent as a term of comparison. For millions of years, humanity has lived with the idea that the polarized terms in nature and existence are bare facts to be assumed as such unless one becomes insane. The revolution announced by Marxism claims to be *the* teleological cataclysm; it founds a new world and a new humanity.

The proclamations of the New Testament as recorded above cannot be ranged in either the first or the second category. The main reason for this is that the New Testament vision is not dualistic. The poles present are not two contraries in mutual exclusion. They are not two terms destined for eventual collapse. Male and female, Greek and Jew, slave and master are two realities thrusting towards each other as they find in their opposites that which is lacking in themselves. No slaves without masters, no masters without slaves. No priest-Jew without the Greek-parishioner, no parishioner-Greek without the Jew. Here, neither of the two terms can be complete without its complement. No one can be independent and self-containing. The basic sociological nucleus for Biblical literature is not the individual—male or female—but the union of both in one flesh (cf. Gen. 1:27; 2:23, 24). The difference between sexes, races, economic classes, types of societies is the motor for a movement of communion between "I and Thou." The difference is the condition for each's thrust towards the other. Each pole is conditioned by the other. Each has existence only in relationship to the other. What is true for sex is also true for the other pairs of terms considered by the abovementioned New Testament texts. Therefore, far from being in a distressful enmity facing each other, the poles are in an existential complementarity; they need to encounter in order that the unity may be born.[6] The final expectation, from this perspective, is not that one sex will convert the other to itself, nor that a third sex, a mixture of the former two, shall sometime appear. The expectation is a promise, and, as a promise, contains an actual fulfillment without ever reaching the point where the tension is dissolved.[7] It is in the tension itself that the accomplishment is achieved; it is in the marriage of man and woman that they become "one flesh." Rollo May writes: "we are created as male and female, which leads to perpetual yearning for each other, a thirst for completion which is doomed to be temporary. . . . The existence of maleness and femaleness, seen ontologically, is one expression of this fundamental polarity of all reality. . . . The sex act is the most powerful enactment of relatedness **imaginable.**"[8]

The readers of the New Testament epistles are said to be not any longer *of* the world; but they do live *in* the world. Now, the wordly conditions of existence tend to raise definite doubts whether the "fundamental polarity of all reality" is a creative complementarity. "In the world," the complementarity appears to be only wishful thinking. On the contrary, what is apparent is the enmity between the independent terms cut off from each other by a "dividing wall of hostility." Paul therefore —or one of his disciples—proclaims the transcendent dimension of the unity of the two terms. It is a unity which is communion and not confusion. A unity which is the *movement* of unification and never the static outcome of the movement. "Here there cannot be Greek and Jew, circumcised and uncircumcised, barbarian, Scythian, slave, free man" (Col. 3:10–11); "there is neither male nor female." (Gal. 3:28) But a few lines later in Colossians Paul shows clearly that he was not speaking of a Hegelian synthesis, for he exhorts the wives to be subject to their husbands! (He turns successively to husbands, children, fathers, slaves, and masters; see Col. 3:18ff.) And the text of Romans 10:12—"there is no distinction between Jew and Greek"—occurs right in the midst of the famous passage which speaks of the relationship between Jews and Gentiles and emphasizes the different integrals which characterize them (Rom. 9—11). As for Galatians 3:28, the statement that all people are "one in Christ Jesus" is followed by the affirmation that we all are "Abraham's offspring, heirs according to the promise," a feature which qualifies precisely what kind of unity ours is.

The nations' unity with Israel is in the election of Abraham, who is the father of Israel and the initiator of her history (culminating for Paul in Jesus Christ).

Any holiness of the Gentiles is participation in Israel's history. It thus seems as if the Israel-pole had swallowed up the Gentile-pole in the process. In that case, Paul would hail the newness of time in which "there is neither Jew nor Greek" (Gal. 3:28) because everybody has become Jewish. Such a stand, however, is untenable. On the contrary, it is clear that Paul's contention is precisely that the Gentiles do not need to convert to Judaism in order not to remain "separated from Christ, alienated from the commonwealth of Israel, . . . strangers to the covenants of promise, having no hope and without God in the world." (Eph. 2:12) The unity of Jews and Gentiles is realized in the love of a common treasury, not in the blotting out of their particularities. Male remains forever male, and female remains female. But their unity is achieved in their common love, in the very movement which thrusts them towards each other and both towards their common destiny. Jew remains Jew, and Gentile remains Gentile. The Jews always remain "first," be it for chastisement or for "glory and honor and peace." (Rom. 2:9–11; Amos 3:2) Their advantage is "Much in every way. To begin with, the Jews are entrusted with the oracles of God" (Rom. 3:1–4), and "as regards election they are beloved for the sake of their forefathers." (Rom. 11:28) As for the Gentiles, they "have received the spirit of adoption . . . [so as to become] children of God, and if children, then heirs, heirs of God and fellow heirs with the Messiah, provided we suffer with him in order that we may also be glorified with him." (Rom. 8:15–17, my translation)

The New Testament does not proclaim the reversal of an "old" economy. Its eschatology is not Marxist but Biblical, i. e., the unity of the sexes, the races, the classes has always been present and affirmed since the beginning by Israel, and is now, according to the early Church, manifested in the world. The Christian is not invited to maintain, against all logic, that "there is neither male nor female" in physical reality, as if these old phenomena had disappeared as culturally bound to an outdated age. No one is asked to fall into the naive and destructive illusion that "there is neither slave nor free" anymore in our world. Such a puerility has had the same disastrous consequences on the economic, political, and intellectual level in the Western world as the modern confusion between the sexes in the psychic realm. If there are no slaves anymore in our "Christian" society, there would be no reason why one should attempt to liberate them. In fact, a misinterpretation of Paul's statements on the encounter between the poles has led Christians to refuse reality for the sake of the ideal. In other words, the Christian Church has been permeated with the fatal denial of matter. Everything has been "spiritualized" so that one is able to juggle with paradoxes: there is neither male nor female, but in the concreteness of life the female is looked down on as a second-rate human being. There is neither Jew nor Gentile, but in the terrible matter of history, the Jews are martyred by the Gentiles "simply because their name is Isaac." Puerility is always on the verge of becoming hypocrisy; and hypocrisy on the brink of becoming bloody cruelty. The "Christian" centuries sadly illustrate that process. It is therefore an important and ceaseless task to purify our world view of all traces of dualism, following in this the perennial example of Israel. Moreover, the dualism must not be merely solved theoretically, spiritually, or eschatologically. The communion of the two terms in the polarity is achieved in the concreteness of our world and our time, or else it is never realized. But when all escapes into metaphysics or "green pastures" are thwarted, we inevitably realize that, in point of fact, there are here and now Jews *and* Greeks, men *and* women, free people *and* slaves, blacks *and* whites, lunatics *and* sages, children *and* adults, etc.

So we must pose the question: is Paul's proclamation of the unity of creation a mere yearning, or the replacement of the real by the fantastic? Since the birth of the Christian Church, everyone taking her message seriously has had to struggle with her proclamation that the kingdom of God is already present among us, and even that resurrection is an event of the past rather than the future.[9] Does it make sense? Is there not an irremediable opposition between the Church's statement and a daily history marked by war, famine, pollution, failure, death? Martin Buber movingly exclaims: "Standing bound and shack-

led in the pillory of the human race, we demonstrate with the
bloody body of our people the unredeemedness of the world."[10]
And he also says that the Jew, "as part of the world, experiences,
perhaps more intensely than any other part, the world's lack of
redemption. He feels this lack of redemption against his skin,
he tastes it on his tongue, the burden of the unredeemed world
lies on him. Because of this almost physical knowledge of his, he
cannot concede that the redemption has taken place; he knows
that it has not."[11] The Christian scholar J. Coert Rylaarsdam
agrees from a morphological point of view: "Christian an-
nouncement of fulfilment seems unrealistic. . . . history and the
world are unredeemed because they do not embody God's rule
of justice. This is true; the Christian must admit it."[12]

Here again, the real opposition is between static and dynamic. In the marriage of a man and a woman, everything
witnesses against their unity; he is what she is not and she is
what he is not. Physiologically, psychologically, spiritually, their
feelings, their reactions are irreconcilable. But unity is impossible between two similar terms. Male and male cannot become
one. Only contrariety is the source of unity, because something,
anything, can only exist when confronted by its contrary. When
they are in confrontation, each's indigence appears in broad,
full daylight.

We are thus dealing with an either-or situation. One can
indeed immobilize the two poles' irreducibility and indulge in
the luxury of speaking "spiritually" of their unity, on the model
of a Greek ideal. Or one can maintain that their irreducibility
is transcended by the dynamic thrust which makes them reach
out towards each other. True, statically speaking, the poles remain in a radical otherness in their face-to-face opposition. But
this observation—which is the result of analysis—is only par-
tially true. Kinetically, there is *between* the poles a "magnetic
field," a reaching out, an encounter; there is what is called in
Hebrew *"Emtsa"* (in between) of which the Maharal of Prague
spoke.[13] The *Emtsa* is the medium of the covenant, the inter-
mediation between I and Thou. The Maharal writes: "Any unity
is in the center, the extremities are divided, the center alone is

One." In a Midrash recorded in *j. Taanit* 68c, it is said that when God handed down the tables of the Law to Moses, the length of two palms was in God's hands, the length of two other palms in Moses' hands, and in the middle the length of two palms remained uncovered. These latter, said the Maharal, are the symbol of the ongoing *process* of the covenant-making. God's hands and human hands are not contiguous, for if they were, nothing could make them communicate. Not being in tension towards each other, they would be content with their juxtaposition.

Thus, dynamically, the two poles are perfecting each other through love. They unceasingly find their unity in letting the "other," in Buber's words, "fill the horizon."

Love has no place in the archetypical, dualistic *Weltanschauung,* as presented above. Nor does it have any role in the Marxist eschatology. In the former, the two poles never meet. In the latter, the two poles are reduced to a *tertium quid,* a synthesis of thesis and antithesis. But this is in fact a confession of impotence: in the present economy, no coming together of polarized terms is conceivable. Eventually one of them must destroy the other and, in the process, be itself transformed into something else. This is similar to the belief of cannibals that they are different after having absorbed the flesh and soul of their foes.

A transformation also occurs when "Jews" and "Greeks" enter into communion with each other. The Jews are no longer the same as they were; neither are the Greeks. But here there is no "cannibalism." The married man is not the bachelor he was, and the matron is not the virgin of old. The difference in them is produced by the dynamic relationship with the opposite pole which becomes a partner in the process. Man, from *na'ar,* becomes *īsh* in his relationship with an *'almah,* who becomes *ishshah* (woman). Let me quote Rollo May here again:

> No woman, supposedly, has stepped off the boat at Athos since the twelfth century. But the monks themselves had taken on the gestures, the ways of talking, walking and carrying themselves of women. . . . when there are no

> women present, there is no accent on acting male and
> vice versa; we become more masculine when there are
> women around, and they are more feminine. *The two
> sexes have the function of accentuating the characteris-
> tics of the opposite one. . . . [the] sexes seem to ignite each
> other, offering a vitality and power—and even better
> ideas.*[14]

I will wait until the next chapter to discuss *in what* the
Church and the Synagogue are affected by each other. Suffice
it here to focus attention on the *how* of their mutual transformation. So far, I have drawn a clear-cut parallelism in the relationship between all the poles listed in the Pauline texts quoted
above. The polarity male-female proved especially useful for
our purpose. We now reach the point where the identity of
process becomes the most significant. As a matter of fact, in the
communion of male and female, the aim is for both to become
at last what they actually are—man becomes really Man and
woman really Woman. In the office of the Synagogue, men
thank God to have been created men, and women to have been
created what they are. Both say it at the same time and acknowledge by the same token that "they are what they are"
thanks to the other sex. Each needs the other with the same
intensity and with the same outcome of becoming a fulfilled
human being "in the image of God." But we must go further in
this respect. It is important to realize that maleness and femaleness embody two complementary vocations, two complementary dynamic functions of a single entity whose very *raison
d'être* is to be in relationship with God. In the covenant between the Creator and the creature, "man" (*īsh;* Adam) is the
name given to the function/vocation of forwarding *the event* of
the encounter. In Judaism as in Christianity, the husband is
priest in his family, or "Christ" vis-à-vis his spouse who in turn
is "the Church" (cf. Eph. 5:22ff.). As a corollary, "woman"
(*ishshah;* Eve) is the name given to the function/vocation of
grounding the event of the encounter into its appropriate *institution.* She allows the event to become incarnate; she, like
Mary pregnant with the Holy Spirit, harbors and nests in the

fiber of her flesh and body—extended to the confines of her household or clan—the spiritual power coming from God, whether it comes directly or, more commonly, through the priestly action of the family head. Both the event and the institution go together and are inseparable, like life and existence. As the latter comes after and is conditioned by the former, so woman is created to be the helpmate of man, and not conversely (cf. Gen. 2:18).[15]

Similarly for Israel and the nations. In the loving relationship which unites them and "breaks down the dividing wall of hostility" between them, the issue is for the latter to become "members of the household of God." (Eph. 2:19) Israel remains forever the name and the reality of God's people. The Gentiles in the New Testament are invited, not to constitute a rival community over against the Jewish people, but to become "fellow citizens with the saints." (Eph. 2:19) They are to become Israel with Israel, or, as Galatians 6:16 puts it, "the Israel of God." To cite once again the metaphor used above, the nations' vocation is to tend towards the day when Israel, their male-partner, fulfills his identification with God, becoming holy as God is holy. As for the nations, they then cover themselves with the mantle of the Jews and minister to *them* (cf. 2 Kings 19:19).

How then will the fact that there is neither Jew nor Greek be manifested in the world? Only by proving existentially that the God they both worship is the God of *Israel.* The Church will find here her only *raison d'être.* She will even be, like Aaron for his brother Moses, the prophetic mouth of Israel in proclaiming the good news that the world's "time of service is accomplished, that its guilt is paid off, that it has received of the Lord's hand double for all its sins" (cf. Isa. 40:2). Is there another answer to Martin Buber's accusation that the Church is a self-centered, self-deifying reality, because she does not listen to God's voice but indulges in a "monologue of alternating voices with herself"?[16] The Church will show by her doctrine and by her life that she intends, on the contrary, to be in dialogue with the living God, the God of *Israel.* If it were not so, "our preaching is in vain and . . . [our] faith is in vain. . . . we are of all men most

to be pitied." (1 Cor. 15:14, 19) We would deprive ourselves of
the right of citizenship with the saints in the name of (as Buber
put it) that "image of Jesus which has conquered the soul of
peoples and has transformed it."

That distorted image of the "factual Jesus" has been in-
formed by a philosophy diametrically opposed to the genuine
Christian kerygma rooted in Judaism. The established Church
has been trapped into a Neoplatonic expression of her faith.
This fact has to be traced back to the time when the Christians
of the first centuries had to speak the language of their Hellenized audiences. The very necessity of speaking Greek entailed
far-reaching consequences. The categories, more than just the
words, had to be translated. True, as long as the contact with
the "Twelve" in Jerusalem was kept alive, the originality of the
message conveyed in the new language was also protected. But
as soon as the ties with Palestine were severed, the "translation"
progressively ceased and the criteria themselves became
Greek, not any longer Jewish. The evolution started early,
around the time of the canonization of a "New Testament" as
we saw above (chapter 6, appendix B). But it was especially in
the fourth century C.E. that the Christian Church began to
appear as a full-fledged institution with a deep political rootage
in the Roman Empire. From a "sect" (Jewish or anti-Jewish
depending upon the point of view), it became an independent
religion. The Neoplatonic influence was present everywhere, so
much so that St. Augustine, for example, polemicized against it.
Christendom has travestied the dialogue with the factual Jesus
—who sends us back to the gracious covenant of God with Israel
—into an awestruck contemplation of a religious hero superbly
alone in performing the labors of a new Hercules. In fact, despite the isolated phenomenon of anchoritism, the "Church"
has by and large forgotten the wilderness, as if the promised
land were a static reality separable from the suffering of making
it true in day-to-day life. Christendom has settled, it has refused
to lose its life; it has refused to suffer. It has boasted of being
"God's heir and Christ's fellow heir" (Rom. 8:17, my translation), but has obliterated the rest of the sentence: "provided

that we share his sufferings now in order to share his splendor hereafter." It has carefully forgotten that it is truly itself only when, like its mother Israel, it is laboring "in all manner of service in the field." (Exod. 1:14, KJV)

Contrary to the Churchly Establishment, the Jews have always appeared as a foreign body in the world. Unwilling (or psychologically unable?) to compromise with the crimes of the world, they had to affirm themselves over against the complacent ideologies of the nations. By their very presence in the midst of the other nations, they wittingly or unwittingly abolish the illusion of the heathen systems. That is why Daniel is denounced as an outlaw although he continues his normal existence. His keeping to his way of being constantly and faithfully is readily construed as resistance to the system (Dan. 6).[17] Jesus, later, is condemned as *lēstēs,* bandit. For to *be* Israel is a movement in history; the Jew knows that the accomplishment of life "depends not upon man's will or exertion, but upon God's mercy." (Rom. 9:16) What the Babylonian sages, representing all the nations, reproach Daniel-Israel for is his hope. This is sufficient reason to "cast him into the den of lions." The *raison d'état* cannot be relativized for anyone, for fear that it would be demonstrated that it is what it is, an enslaving myth, a trap into which the initiator of the ideology himself falls (cf. Dan. 6:15, 17, 19, etc.). *"Le pitre ne rit pas":* the buffoon—and the buffoon's flatterers—do not laugh; they must keep up the rules of the game—even if the game is meaningless. Anything is preferable to the emptiness they discover in their own souls.

In fact, the Jews embarrass the others in their rush for *panem et circenses.* They refuse to "play" with the others and, by the same token, they show that the game is empty and cruel. Theoretically, one can imagine a game where not everyone has to take part. Practically, history proves that this does not happen. Woe to any who make themselves conspicuous by their oddity, even if, like Daniel, they do so in a peaceful manner and give no active offense. Such people must be sacrificed on the altar of the general mediocrity.[18] To stick to one's oddity entails the sacrifice of one's self.

Again, I wonder if Christendom can recognize itself in this picture. I wonder whether it has become—"with the saints and members of the household of God"—the exorciser of all debasing myths and slogans, or whether it has not rather become a convenient and comfortable institution of the state. All the *"Gott mit uns,"* the "In God we trust," the flags in church buildings, the "anti-Communism crusades" reveal much about the compromises with the "Dariuses" of the present. To be sure, God declares that he will leave " 'seven thousand in Israel, [namely] all the knees that have not bowed to Baal, and every mouth that has not kissed him.' " (1 Kings 19:18) This very holiness which the true Church lives—as the Synagogue, voluntarily or involuntarily, whether this matters—consists in the perpetual self-sacrifice of the innocent in conformity with the holiness-sacrifice of Israel since the beginning. For it is the same sacrifice, unique and valid "once and for all" for the salvation of the world. At the beginning of the Second World War, Karl Barth exclaimed, "How is it that the Nazis do not understand that the suffering of the Jews is the suffering of Christ?" By undergoing the same painful struggle as the Nazarene—as the corporate personality of Israel—the Church will reach the same victory acquired by the Messiah of *Israel,* in the name of *Israel,* and for *Israel.* Is there another "bringing near" (cf. Eph. 2:13); is there any other partaking in the "commonwealth of Israel" (Eph. 2:12); is there any other "fellow citizenship with the saints" (cf. Eph. 2:19)? No. Israel remains here and now and forever the touchstone, the criterion, the rock, the foundation, the cornerstone, the rock of scandal: all of these terms also depict Christ, because Christ is none other than the fulfillment in his person of the vocation of his people. A vocation accomplished *and* accomplishing itself, a history victoriously finished *and* still happening, a suffering fully sufficient, and yet still completing itself (cf. Col. 1:24). Israel-Church—the two are now but one (Eph. 2:14) because the latter has meaning only in relation to the former, and the former only attains its object truly in the latter.

There is no more Jew or Greek *here and now,* because the

Church (and to the extent to which the Church) acts the action of Israel, the Israel to whom "belong the sonship, the glory, the covenants, the giving of the law, the worship, and the promises; to them belong the patriarchs, and of their race, according to the flesh, is the Christ." (Rom. 9:4–5) Into this family the Church has been "adopted" (Rom. 8:15, 23; Gal. 4:5). Adopted, not only by the Father, so that it would be possible to conceive that the adopted child might eventually supplant and replace the flesh-and-blood heir, but adopted by Israel as well (cf. Eph. 2; Rom. 9—11). The Gentiles have been "grafted" onto the pure olive tree and "made partakers of the root and the sap of the olive tree." (Rom. 11:17, my translation) It is therefore vital for the Church to remember in time and out of time the warning of the apostle: "it is not you that support the root, but the root that supports you." (Rom. 11:18) Paul, in Romans, does not speak of the passing of the gracious election of God from one nation to another, but of the reception of a grace similarly granted to Jews and Gentiles, i. e., as an undeserved gift. It is a common mistake to read Paul as if he were focusing the interest on *the elected*—so that the latter could presume on their merits. This misreading of the texts leads to the vain discussion on the respective qualities of the Jews and the non-Jews in God's opinion. Nothing can be more presumptuous. In fact, Paul's emphasis is on *the Elector.* God, according to Paul, shows his sovereign liberty when he says, " 'I will have mercy on whom I have mercy, and I will have compassion on whom I have compassion.' So it depends not upon man's will or exertion, but upon God's mercy." (Rom. 9:15–16; cf. Exod. 33:19) Paul's statement leaves no room for ambiguity. But a few verses later, the parable used by Paul opens up the way to misinterpretation. One is tempted to allegorize and, since the apostle is speaking of the potter having full rights over the clay for molding the same lump into "one vessel for beauty and another for menial use" (Rom. 9:21), tempted to identify the former and the latter vessels respectively with the non-Jews and the Jews. Apart from the fact that a parable is no allegory, such an exegesis goes directly against the intention of Paul, explicitly stated in verses

23–24 (my emphasis): "What if *God,* desiring to show *his* wrath and to make known *his* power, has endured with much patience the vessels of wrath made for destruction, in order to make known the riches of *his* glory for the vessels of mercy, which *he* has prepared beforehand for glory, even us whom *he* has called, *not from the Jews only but also from the Gentiles?*" The argument is clearly centered on God's unconditional freedom to choose whomsoever he wants and, therefore, to constitute his beloved People with Jews and Gentiles alike. This is a truth which is exemplified throughout the Hebrew Scriptures but which needed to be unequivocally restated when, with an unexpected suddenness, the "good tidings" reached the "coastlands" of the entire world.

There is therefore an unbreakable unity, not only between the Church and her Christ, but also and primarily between Christ and Israel. As the Messiah is the common denominator between the Jews and the Gentiles, he makes of them both "in himself one new man in place of the two . . . thereby bringing the hostility to an end." (Eph. 2:15–16) In effect, it means that to the extent that the Church's claim to be one with her Christ proves true, she is also one with the Israel of God.

It is out of the question here to give a complete exposition of the New Testament's Christology, showing the fulfilling character of the Nazarene's mission. Let me simply recall briefly several facts in this respect.

1. Jesus was a Jew, born from Jews, in Palestine, "when Quirinius was governor of Syria." (Luke 2:2)

2. He lived in his country, among his people, limiting his mission to " 'the lost sheep of the house of Israel.' " (Matt. 15:24)[19]

3. He chose twelve messengers, called disciples, according to the number of the Israelite tribes (cf. Matt. 19:28).

4. The different choices he made during his ministry make sense only because they fulfill the Scriptures of Israel (cf. John 19:28).

5. He spoke to his fellow Jews in their own terms, confining himself strictly to their particular categories of thinking, and sharing their *Weltanschauung* (cf. Matt. 5:17ff.).

6. He was judged according to Jewish standards by the Sanhedrin (although the crucifixion was a Roman torture).

7. Jesus' disciples were all Jews and the primitive Church was entirely Jewish. Primitive Christianity was merely a Judaism living in its fulfillment and carefully and in fact painfully drawing out the consequences of the accomplishment. It was over this particular point that all the divisions appeared in the Church, and not principally on the unquestioned fact that Jesus embodied the omega point of Judaism. Only later on in history did the schism *par excellence* between the Judeo-Christians and the Pagano-Christians occur. Then, what had before been a family quarrel became a division between two independent bodies, almost two religions. Strictly speaking, one could say that the Church's span of life was only a few years. Since then, the agonized invalid has survived thanks to medical devices. The diagnosis is simple enough, however: " 'No one can serve two masters' "—in the present case, Israel's living God and a Neoplatonic idol usurping the attributes of the former—" 'for either he will hate the one and love the other, or he will be devoted to the one and despise the other.' " (Matt. 6:24)

We are thus forced to make a distinction between those who share in the usurpation we just mentioned, and reduce the living God to a ludicrous god of success worshiped by the Establishment, and, on the other hand, a remnant existentially committed to the God of failure.[20] No compromise can ever be achieved between these two radically opposed options.

The same sap flows through the fibers of Israel and those who are grafted onto it, to the point that the fruits of the wild olive tree become those of the cultivated olive tree.[21] That is why the Jews are always and forever "first." This last word is important in the New Testament vision of the new economy in Christ (cf. Rom. 1:16; 2:9–10). Michaelis[22] gives to this term the sense of *"vor allem"* (before all), and in another context, in Matthew 6:33, the meaning of the word can even cover *"nur"* (only)! Where Israel is concerned, we cannot lay this last meaning aside lightly. In fact, all is *only* Israel's; the good news is *only* for the twelve tribes. It is *only* to these that "the sonship, the glory, the covenants, the giving of the law, the worship, and the promises . . . [and even] the Christ" belong (Rom. 9:4–5). Once more we face here the "exclusiveness" of the texts of the Hebrew Scriptures, but, as we saw earlier, this is precisely the token of the universality of the love of God. Thus, if the one-time heathens are also at the benefit of the inheritance of Israel, it is because they have taken "hold of the robe of a Jew, saying, 'Let us go with you, for we have heard that God is with you.' " (Zech. 8:23)

This respective place of "Israel-as-first" (i. e., God's children of Jewish origin) and "Israel-as-second" (i. e., God's adopted heirs of Gentile stock) is the one that God has laid down for all eternity. It is not, and never will be, questioned because the story of salvation is one. Nothing in the heavens or on the earth will ever come to break the covenant of God with us through *Israel,* through the fulfillment of the Law brought about by the Christ in the *name of all Israel.*

8. Synagogue and Church

The previous chapter has emphasized the mutuality of Israel and Christendom. Christ, said the author of Ephesians 2, has torn down the wall of hostility between Jews and Gentiles, "for he is ... [their] peace, who has made ... [them] both one." (Eph. 2:14) There is neither Jew nor Gentile!

This joyous proclamation of the early Church, however, did not find substantiation in its institutions. Instead of becoming the locus of the communion between the circumcised and the uncircumcised, the Church has historically confronted the Synagogue and both have lived for centuries side by side in mutual ignorance, distrust, and sometimes hatred. Reality, therefore, seems to be irreducible to the Pauline notion (which I reassessed in chapters 6 and 7), and that notion appears to be dependent on wishful thinking.

This chapter's aim is to get a closer look into this question. Can the Church actually ignore the Synagogue and still be the Church? Can the Synagogue actually ignore the Church and still be the Synagogue? What is the theological and existential content of the complementarity of the two "brought together" through the Christ event alleged by the New Testament? What is the indispensable role of the Synagogue for the sake of the Church? What role must the Church play for the sake of the Synagogue? Put in the negative, how does the Church relinquish her *raison d'être* when cut from her Jewish root as presented and represented by the Synagogue? How does the Synagogue sterilize her vocation when not concerned with the Church?

This chapter prolongs the lines sketched in the previous one, and tries to show how in the concreteness of their existence the Church and Synagogue are bound together in God's plan and for eternity.

If one had to say in a few words what the *raison d'être* of the Church is, perhaps the best summation would be the last statement of the Crucified: "all is accomplished." The Church is the living proclamation of the flawless fulfillment of all things. But this remains extremely vague as long as it is not specified what we are to understand by the words "all things." And, to our shame, it is precisely in that unspecified "accomplishment" that, much too often, the Church claims to live today. "All" then becomes a category, the "idea" of totality. So that the more we would attempt to specify the content of "all," the more we limit its bearing.

But a "spiritual" accomplishment is a vague philosophy negating the evidence and directing the whims of popular hope toward an unsubstantial future, fruit of a misled imagination. For no honest student of the New Testament can seriously claim that Jesus meant this in uttering his "all is fulfilled." To confuse Jesus with a Greek philosopher speaking only of the world of ideas is the worst possible misunderstanding of the Nazarene.

One must, however, balance this pessimistic picture with some encouraging elements. In the first place, there is, at the level of the local church, a new desire for being exposed to the truth, even when it is not all rosy and flattering. Indeed, such a book as this could not have any chance of being read by my fellow Christians were it not for that new uncompromising spirit in the Church today. Our time witnesses the collapse of a great number of idols, the dismantling of many hoaxes. Inevitably this process of demythologization and of demystification has also permeated the Churchly milieux. A new world is in gestation and, at least in this country, the Church has decided to be instrumental in bringing forth the new era.

I have all along emphasized the necessity for Christians to rediscover (and recover) their Jewish origins and belongingness. In this perspective, one must mention the declaration of the Council of Vatican II on the Jews, for it remains almost without parallel in other Christian confessions. (A noticeable exception: the Dutch Reformed Church.) Some Protestant individuals are also pointing in the right direction. So much so that, because of them and thanks to the *brochette* of Jewish giants such as Franz Rosenzweig, Martin Buber, Abraham Heschel, Emil Fackenheim, André Neher, Elie Wiesel, and others who have become the seed of a renewed Judaism, Synagogue and Church are today, for the first time in sixteen or seventeen centuries, in dialogue. On a spiritual level this fact is the most significant event in this century. Today, Synagogue and Church are no longer the constituencies they used to be, and it is hard to characterize in the present tense their respective stands. In point of fact, both live today in an intermediary period of time. They are *already* different from what they were yesterday, and *not yet* identical with their tomorrow's form towards which they are striving. This, of course, adds considerably to the difficulty of rightly appreciating the present stance of Synagogue and Church. One can no longer state that Synagogue and Church have made the most of their separation and that, sadly, they glory in it and find their self-justification there. Such a judgment was true until very recently, but it is no longer tenable. More and more, Synagogue and Church are discovering that Franz Rosenzweig was insightful when speaking of the "complementary role of the Church and Judaism." He wrote:

> before God, then, Jew and Christian both labor at the same task. He cannot dispense with either. He has set enmity between the two for all time, and withal has most intimately bound each to each. . . . The truth, the whole truth, thus belongs neither to them [Christians] nor to us [Jews]. For we too, though we bear it within us, must for that very reason first immerse our glance into our own interior if we would see it, and there, while we see the Star, we do not see—the rays. And the whole truth would demand not only seeing its light but also what was illuminated by it. They [the Christians], however, are in any event already destined for all time to see what is illuminated, and not the light.[1]

So our task from the start is difficult and ambiguous. In order to be fair in judgment, each must step up on the other's level and appreciate the situation from inside, not from outside. There is no doubt that a large number of Christians have so outrageously exaggerated the "legalism" of the Synagogue that it is legitimate for the Jews not to recognize themselves in such a distorted image. It is also understandable that Christian rebuttals, shooting so far beyond the target, fall ludicrously useless— if they do not become criminal weapons in "Christian" pogroms. Against such a background there is no harder task on the part of Gentiles of good will than to have the boldness to call to the Synagogue's attention the inner criticism offered to her by her own children. I do not refer only to Jesus—certainly the most radical by far among the critics "from inside"—but also Hillel, Akiba, the Baal Shem Tov and his disciples, the mystics, Martin Buber, and so many others. All of them, each in his own terms, recalled to Israel that "shabbat has been created for man, not man for shabbat." The necessary strictness in keeping the *mitsvoth* must be placed in its real perspective of liberating people, not enslaving them to another determinism as despotic as the "Greek" one. But a new era has begun and the recent events of Auschwitz and the State of Israel press hard on the Synagogue for a reappraisal of her essence and message. My contention is, as it has been all along in this book, that Israel, that all people, achieve their authentic identity in self-sacrifice for the love of God. This is the true fulfillment of the Torah.

Nothing can be more concrete and more down-to-earth. Nothing is less esoteric and "particularist" in a restrictive sense. And it is precisely at this point that the Synagogue is the necessary guardian of the Church. She recalls to her "daughter" that what is important is not primarily a harmoniously balanced systematic theology. What is capable of healing the world is not an impressive set of dogmas. For nothing falling short of sacrificial love can really bring about a new creation. Without Golgotha and without Auschwitz the world and humanity are perhaps liked but not loved, objects of sympathy but not integrated, embraced but not fertilized. The Synagogue, martyred for more than twenty centuries, prevents the Church from flirting with the world, forcing her to confront this world and to incarnate herself instead of hovering over our quest and suffering. She calls Christians to leave the realm of dualistic religious ideas where the "soul" has become an abstraction opposed to a "flesh" which is sadly material.[2] The Synagogue rightly presses the issue of fulfillment as advocated by the Church. What is an accomplishment which would leave the world unchanged? What is a blessing which could only be defined in "spiritual" terms? A blessing must be sensitive, creative of new life, or it does not exist. The problem is not the after-death but the *hic et nunc,* the here and now, of humanity. Here and now, in the human integrity, everything takes place, or else nothing takes place. If it is true that the reign of God has been inaugurated by Jesus of Nazareth, the effects must surely be felt: it is here and now that there must be no more wars, famines, illnesses, death.[3]

No criticism can be more appropriate than this one, and the Church stands or falls on this very issue. In a time such as this, which is unparalleled in history for its wars, injustices, natural and fabricated catastrophes, this question is to be taken more seriously than ever. Isn't it to be wondered whether Christianity makes any difference today in human behavior or in international mores? *Did* the coming of the Christian Christ and his official acknowledgment by millions of human beings give history a new thrust? The "all is fulfilled" of Jesus seems to have solved no problems and to be thus a *petitio principii* only capable of luring naive believers and providing an opiate to the populace.

On a more sophisticated level, however, one still finds many Christians understanding the "all is accomplished" as a juridical nominalistic, exterior statement. They have no ethical investment in it, considering that they are automatically at its benefit as long as they intellectually claim to be. The relationship with the fulfillment remains on a mythical level. Even Søren Kierkegaard was not immune to such a misconception. He wrote: "All the historical, social, effects of our actions are indifferent.

The Universe is in vain. State means number; Christianity means individuality. Both concepts stand in opposition to each other."[4] Faith, in this view, consists of leaving generality for the sake of particularity. One may wonder what Kierkegaard would have said about Auschwitz, Oradour, Hiroshima, My Lai, and the U.S.S.R. concentration camps.

Over against the Christian spiritualization or individualism, the Synagogue's question is all the sharper. What does it mean for all people here and now that the kingdom of God has drawn near in the person of Christ? The problem is complex and its solution requires in the first place a double rejection: on the one hand, of the widespread nominalism among Christians; on the other hand, and correspondingly, of the widespread concept among Jews of the automatism of the messianic era. The latter stance expects that the Messiah will establish, once and for all and independent of any human participation, the kingdom of God on earth. When this is done, everyone will automatically be at the benefit of this kingdom and the effects of sin will, no less automatically, disappear. *Shalom* will then be installed and will remain forever, unquestioned and unthreatened. This Jewish concept is not new and constitutes probably one of the main reasons why Jesus did not use the title "Messiah" in speaking about himself.[5] He definitely did not understand his vocation in terms of taking the place and the responsibility of anyone else. He was not to live, respond to his and Israel's God, suffer and die, *instead of* his People. The Nazarene understood his People's vocation as leading to the ultimate. He considered that to the totality of God's gift, all people had to respond with the totality of their lives. It is only in this sense that his death can be considered as in the place of and for the sake of his People. As Isaiah 53:10 says, *"Im tasim asham naphsho yir'eh zerah yaarich yamim"* (*"If* his life offers restitution, then he will see a progeny, he will prolong his days," my translation). Here, against all idea of automatism, we find the full participation of the "choir" confessing God's pleasure in him whom they first thought rejected, stricken, smitten, and afflicted. Without the People's confession, the Servant's sacrifice remains invalid, a total failure because its message does not reach anybody. The remnant or the whole of Israel speaking in Isaiah 53 raises the dead Servant, restores him to life. Through their confession, the Servant lives, and, moreover, he "sees a progeny, he prolongs his days." His sacrifice is his triumph. His death is his life. The living one is not the coward Pilate who "washes his hands," the living one is not the torturer in the camps.

The kingdom of God is no "green pasture" where one drinks milk and smokes cigars, it is no repose for Israel and the world, it is no victory *after* the battle. The reign of God is his innocence *(tsedaqa)* which is chosen as such, assumed by and incarnated in the innocent man *(tsadiq)*. When people (and even one man would be enough—this is the argument of the epistle to the Hebrews) realize that, the reign of God is actually enacted on earth. This is humanhood in its full sense.

What is at stake therefore is no change in our environmental conditions which would spare us personal total commitment and enactment. For "man carries within himself the potentiality of redemption. . . . The logical point could . . . be made that the future eventuality of redemption at once presupposes present unredeemedness and the ever-immanent possibility of redemption taking place."[6] This dialectical point made by A. Roy Eckhardt deserves to be pursued. Redemption supposes unredeemedness. It is part of Christian and Jewish misconception to relegate to a dead past or to the transient present, respectively, the unredeemedness of the world. In point of fact, redemption is a process, a dynamic encounter with the unredeemed. Jesus does not present himself so much as *the Redeemer,* but rather as the way for people to find redemption. First, chronologically, Jesus pointed to total love as *the* way; then, under the pressure of events and because there is no "word" without its incarnation (no artistic work not filled with the artist's soul and life), he himself had to embody his own predication and become in his own existence and in his own death the way about which he was speaking. When the Jewish primitive Church came to refer to him as the Redeemer, the title was naturally—in a Semitic way—understood as descriptive of an action, a movement, a history. Jesus was the Redeemer because his redemption was in process, just as he was the Messiah because his "messianizing" of the world was in progress. And since Redeemer or Messiah was not a title of someone limited in time by his birth at the one end and his death at the other, the Church had to proclaim his "preexistence" and his "post-existence," understood as the preexistence and the post-existence of the redemption performed by him as the Redeemer. She said, with John, "In the beginning was the Word . . . And the Word . . . dwelt among us." She also had to announce his "resurrection," because he was not *a* transient way to redemption but *the* way, as much as love is not *a* way but *the* way. The Nazarene was for her the epitome of messiahships, he was *the* Messiah, in whom all the Messiahs of history find their fulfilled image. He was more Abraham than Abraham, more Moses than Moses, more David than David, more Zerubbabel than Zerubbabel, more Akiba or the *"Lamed Vav"* or the People of Israel than they are, because he gave for them, in their name and with them, the ultimate response to God. He was thus more Jew than any Jew. He was the Central Jew, and therefore the Central Man. "The Christian has no alternative but to testify that for him the preeminent fulfillment of Israel's universalism takes place *through the Jew,* Jesus of Nazareth."[7]

Jesus is his People, Israel of yesterday, today, and tomorrow. Daniel 7, speaking of the Son of Man, shows the essential unity between him and all the "saints." There is identity between the individual Messiah and the collective Messiah. That is why, at one of the peaks of the gospel, there is the declaration of Jesus that " ' "as you did it to one of the least of these my brethren, you did it to me." ' " (Matt. 25:40) Granted, the Church is right in thinking, in this respect, of the poor, the wretched, she encounters every day. But she ought to realize that the poor and the wretched are "Christ-like" only because their predicament is on the model, so to speak, of Israel's historical plight. So the alien *(ger; toshav)* in Israel is the object of particular care in the Torah, because Israel is the alien *par excellence* in the world.

There is no privileged social class in the Bible, but a participation in or a rejection of the choice Israel incarnates.[8]

It is to be noted that in the context of the judgment as described in Matthew 25, a question spontaneously springs from the mouth of those who are judged (25:37, my translation): "When did we see you hungry and feed you, or thirsty and give you something to drink?" The question is retrospective, for the scene presented by Matthew brings us to the end of time, " 'When the Son of man comes in his glory, and all the angels with him.' " (25:31) It is therefore normal that those who are judged speak of their existence in the past tense, "when did we see," for, in fact the whole course of history is in question. It is thus on actual historical and ethical actions that all are judged, for it is here and now that all are revealing their ultimate choice. The *telos* is therefore both behind us and ahead of us. "When did we see you?" is the type of question one finds in prophetic narrations. Its tense marks the discrepancy between the event as seen by God as having already occurred, and as not yet experienced by us. For the Nazarene, the *telos* is "at hand" in anyone's act of feeding or clothing another. This is what brings time up to its fulfillment. Here again, Jesus is totally Jewish-minded, for in Israel the question is never posed of the salvation or the rejection of anyone independently of historical involvement. Nobody is permanently in the category of "good" or "bad." If the apostle Paul speaks, after the prophet Jeremiah, of "the potter [who] can do as he likes with the clay, [who is] free to mold two vessels out of one lump, one vessel to be treasured, the other for common use" (Rom. 9:21, my translation; cf. Jer. 18:1ff.), it is not with the doctrine of predestination in mind, but with the faith that the all-embracing lordship of God "makes light and creates darkness." (Isa. 45:7, my translation)

The universalism of Israel's vocation expresses itself, among other ways, through an actual judgment on all people's existential choice. For what we do need in our life here and now is an actual redemption, salvation, liberation, and this means also an actual judgment. In Matthew 25, Jesus speaks of a court of

justice where our actions are evaluated because they are here
and now meaningful. This conclusion is far-reaching, for if creation has been made by God in order to stir up a meaningful,
redemptive action of a human community consequently called
Israel, in response to his meaningful, redemptive act, it means
that our judgment is on the basis of our "Jewishness." All our
doings become a testimony to this quality. Nothing is meaningless. Whatever the nature of a human action, a loving encounter
or a murder, there is a divine judgment expressed in it.

Thus also does the Church relate the Synagogue to her role.
She pleads for the Synagogue's taking part in the *Becoming of
God.* She testifies to the Synagogue that the movement is not
valid in itself, for, paradoxically, a movement without thrust
towards the accomplishment is another version of the pagan
cyclical concept of time. As a matter of fact, the Synagogue has
caught herself in an impossible dialectic concerning the coming
of the Messiah. According to the Sages—their memory be
blessed—the Messiah comes for "a generation entirely righteous or for a generation entirely wicked" *(dor kulo zakkai, dor
kulo ḥayav).* [9] This means—as André Neher pointed out in a
speech delivered in 1962 in Antwerp, Belgium—that in the
former case the Messiah is a superfluous luxury, and that in the
latter case the situation is without issue. There will always be a
"last of the just" whose very presence in the "wicked generation" tragically bars the way to the coming of the Messiah and
to the world's salvation! That is why Israel is invited to inter-
cede, after her father Abraham, for Sodom even if eventually
the city is not saved, and perhaps knowing in advance that the
city will not be saved. It thus seems that we are caught in a
circular "no exit" situation. Sodom is doomed to be annihilated,
and the intercession of Abraham does not make any difference,
except maybe to his own soul's welfare. But this is only one
aspect of the reality and it must be balanced with its second
aspect. Abraham's prayer for Sodom cannot remain forever
ineffective. It calls for a surpassing of itself, for no Biblical event
remains static. It is taut towards "the time when God will have
brought the event to its complete fruition" so that it can only

be judged once "the light of its ulterior context, its full meaning, will at last have been made manifest."[10] We are brought out of the impasse of Genesis by Ezekiel 16:53, 55: " 'I will restore their fortunes, . . . the fortunes of Sodom . . . [and] your sisters, Sodom and her daughters shall return to their former estate.' "

The Church acknowledges with humility that she is also Sodom and perhaps moreso than anything else. She rejoices to see Abraham interceding for her and she begs the Synagogue to keep up with the "father of faith" in his unsatisfaction with the destruction of Sodom. On the other hand, the Church reminds the Synagogue of the same thing of which she herself is reminded by the Synagogue: all is not settled, the chips are not down! The warning of the Synagogue was in relation to the "all is accomplished." The Church in her turn recalls that the categories "Jews" and "Gentiles" are complementary and "fluid." Ruth the Moabite becomes the ancestor of David and therefore of the Messiah, and Achan, though a Jew, is stoned to death by his people because he went astray from the covenant with God.

Moreover, if it is true that merely by her presence, by her silent presence, the Synagogue raises a question to Christians, it is also true that the Church constitutes a phenomenon demanding an explanation from the Jews. For the Synagogue cannot remain indifferent to the fact that all nations of the world have heard about Israel's God since the Nazarene's coming. If only from this point of view, Christianity constitutes an important and even decisive messianic fulfillment of Israel's expectation. The least a Jew can say in this connection is that Jesus is "the Messiah of the Gentiles," that he constitutes a development unexpected but nonetheless actual whose bearing cannot be minimized.

No doubt the Jewish author of the epistle to the Ephesians was struck by that very fact; speaking to these Gentiles of Ephesus, he exclaimed that Jesus "is our peace, who has made us both one, and has broken down the dividing wall of hostility." (Eph. 2:14) Church and Synagogue have become the two facets of the same reality; together they have become one new man. Synagogue without Church is a historical abstraction. Church without Synagogue is a stupidity and a swindle. As Dom Emmanuel Lanne writes: "Israel is for the Church a constant reminder of her origins and her destiny. The witness which Israel gives forces the Christians to remember the earthly and therefore essentially transitory character of the cultures with which they are in contact. Only the revelation of that which the Jewish people has been the true recipient of and has transmitted to the Church is a 'culture' worthy of man and of his vocation."[11]

The factual Jewish-Christian unity must eventuate in "apocalypse" (i. e., revelation, epiphany). "When that has taken place, all Israel will be saved." (Rom. 11:26, my translation) This famous statement is no mystical vision on the part of the Jewish apostle. One day, the monument will be unveiled for all eyes to see in this fundamental unity of the two peoples previously separated, the unity of the whole nation of the heirs of God. Between Israel and the Church, the dialogue is permanent. "The Jew," says André Neher paraphrasing Franz Rosenzweig, "is forever the sign given to the Christian that the end is *not yet* there. He is the man of *hope.*"[12] Conversely, the Christians are the sign given to the Jews that the end is *already* with us here and now. Christians are the people of faith as opposed to sight.

This unification of the two who were kept apart by a wall of enmity entails the healing of the cosmos: it definitively bridges the original historical breach between God and his creation. It also brings to fulfillment the history of the covenantal relationship between God and the community of all people. Let us reflect on these two points.

The divine initiative after the "fall" starts with a first paradox when Abram, soon to become Abraham, is called by God and responds to the call. In this universe which has broken itself away from its Creator, and which God wants to reunite to himself, the situation is thus aggravated by a new separation. This step, strange as it seems, emphasizes the effect of sin. Was it not precisely the main outcome of the "fall" to break the oneness of creation? Beforehand, was not everything contained in the primordial unity of God and stamped with the seal of that fundamental unity, in the image of the Creator? Adam is taken from the soil *adamah;* he is animated with the same living breath as all animals. He becomes "one flesh," an *īsh,* with his wife, *ishshah.* But the "fall" brings with it the total isolation of each and every element in creation. From then on each opposes all others. Human sin returns God to his solitude, and the earth, which "was of one language and of one speech," is now "called Babel; because the LORD did there confound the language of all the earth: and from thence the LORD did scatter them [all people] abroad upon the face of all the earth." (Gen. 11:1, 9, KJV)

The division between Israel and the rest of the nations is therefore a scandal, which Paul Démann for instance tries to solve by emphasizing that the author of Israel's election is the One God.[13] This approach is right, but it needs to be complemented by a reflection on the divine goal in selecting Israel. For the one who is chosen is precisely the leaven of the unity of the world. The object, the *telos,* of this choosing of Israel is to allow those who were dispersed to find again their wholeness and their life. Israel is called to be, in the atomized world, the point of junction, the place of reunion: " 'It is too light a thing,' " says God to his People, " 'that you be my servant, to raise up the tribes of Jacob and to restore the preserved of Israel; I will give you as a light to the nations, that my salvation may reach to the end of the earth.' " (Isa. 49:6; cf. 66:18–21; 2:2=Mic. 4:1)

Thus Israel was not chosen *out* of creation in order to constitute a new world for the pleasure of God, but she is the leaven of holiness entrusted with a task for the sake of the whole universe. Israel lives on an earth which becomes holy only by her contact; she lives in a nature which she has the task of regenerating; she uses the language which, in the midst of all the human languages, is destined to name all creatures by their real names. In brief, Israel has as her vocation to be the kingdom of priests in the creation (Exod. 19:6); she is to be the mediator, the Messiah, the word of God to the world, the gift of God to all people. That has been the theme of this book all along.

A second paradox, which depends upon the first one, is that the more Israel is particular, the more that guarantees her universality. In fact, her temptation is not so much to withdraw in a haughty ghetto and to have only contempt for the nations, as to make light of her originality in order to melt, to assimilate into the nations. In the course of her history, Israel needs constantly to be recalled to her unique vocation in the world. Caught between a demanding love and a "natural" desire for rest and repose, Israel lives a tumultuous history, with ups and downs, a history of which each moment only has meaning, value, depth, if the goal, the omega point, is in view. The only hope of the nations is that Israel keep her election, watch over it jealously, and accomplish her exclusiveness totally. For Israel constitutes the channel of grace to support all others. The New Testament announces the good news that the final point has come in the person of Jesus of Nazareth, who personifies the vocation of Israel, the priesthood of Israel, the holiness of Israel, the work of Israel's past, present, and future. Today, the nations are gathered around the twelve priestly tribes, and the twelve are gathered around the central tribe of Levi with the person of the High Priest offering himself as the expiatory victim of sacrifice as their nucleus (cf. Heb. 9:11ff.).

The Jews always come first, for they receive their Messiah directly, while the Gentiles can only receive him mediately, through his people and *as* his people give him to them. This last point is the one guarantee for the non-Jew to encounter the real Jesus and not an imaginary Jesus. This means practically that the Church must revise all her notions, all her dogmas, which may have had their uses, but which do not always correspond to the truth proclaimed by the nation of God. Christ, the Messiah of Israel, has not come to redeem the immortal soul, captive of the debasing prison of the body. Matter, according to the revelation made to the Jews, was created good. By Christ, it is returned to its destination as the temple of the Holy Spirit. Christ has not come to make human history relevant in terms of an eternity which is the negation of time, but to lead history to its accomplishment. He does not withdraw from this world, but brings the whole of humanity's efforts to bear upon the sanctification of all moments and of all things under the sun. He does not internationalize the problem of salvation, but totally fulfills the vocation of Israel and, consequently, becomes in his own person the whole work of his people. It is therefore unthinkable to conceive of the Church as the body which replaces Israel. The Gentiles are grafted onto Israel through a grace which makes them "Semites."[14] The God they have thus learned to serve is not the God of philosophers and scientists, but the God of Jesus Christ, the God of Israel.

This is the golden rule for realizing the unity of the People of God (and they are not synonymous with just the Church, an idea which the documents of the Council of Vatican II still persist in fostering).[15] Granted, the task today, after sixteen to seventeen centuries of shameful divorce, is extremely difficult. The historical schism between the Gentile and the Jewish branches of the Church of the first centuries C.E. has had immeasurable consequences. Not only has the schism yielded the foul, so-called "Christian" anti-Semitism,[16] but it also produced the Church's withdrawal into herself—henceforth the Church too often indulged in a soliloquy, instead of being in dialogue with her Lord and God. Jerusalem disappeared in the night of Christian oblivion and the capital of Christendom drifted to Byzantium, Rome, Moscow, or Geneva.

Paul Démann and Emmanuel Lanne have rightly pointed out that the first schism between Hebrew-Christians and Gentile-Christians laid the foundations for the subsequent schisms in the Church. As long as they lived, the Twelve constituted Christ's "flesh and blood"; they were the navel of the universal Christianity. Paul himself, so often in dissonance with the rest of the apostles, fostered the Twelve's teaching (1 Cor. 11:23; 15:1ff.). But after him the Gentiles went so far as to look at the New Testament for confirmation of their philosophical idealism, of their hatred of matter, of their concept of the soul's immortality. No wonder if ultimately they passed from philosophy to persecution.

The breach, in the midst of God's people, between Church and Synagogue, had incalculable consequences for the Church. It opened the door to all heresies. Not only to crypto-

Marcionism, but to all those infidelities the Church has been dragging behind herself ever since the tragic weakening of the Judeo-Christian branch. One can have the very best systematic theology, but as soon as "Israel according to the flesh" no longer has a place in the Christian vision of history, the root is cut and the tree withers, for one has in fact cut Jesus away from his people.

To the Synagogue, however, Christendom presents a Neo-platonic "Christ," having nothing to do any longer with Israel's Messiah, thus justifying in advance the Synagogue's indignant refusal. By this, I do not mean that a faithful transmission to the Jews of the Nazarene's teaching and vocation would have solved the "Jewish problem" for long. My contention is merely but decidedly that false problems, rivers of blood, swindles and hoaxes, hatred and blindness, pogroms and extermination camps would have been avoided; no less than that.

I do not want here to belittle history. Christianity's entrance into the Greek universe had, from a missionary point of view, far-reaching results. One must recognize that it is only in Jesus of Nazareth's name that Israel's vocation as "light to the nations" is fulfilled, or at least has found an appropriate channel for its accomplishment. But, as we have seen above (chapter 5), fulfillment is not a static concept; it is a thrust, a process always in danger of being short-lived if not kept carefully operative. This actually means that the Church must always return to her life sources. She must reform herself. She must watch over her permanent dialogue with the Jewish people, who, by a paradox-ical and intolerable historical twist, have become foreign to her.

One of the main misunderstandings of the term "Israel" in a "Christianized" world is that it is construed as designating, not the Jewish people in their historical and geographical coordi-nates, but a disincarnated concept. This is especially ironic, for not only has the Church defined herself as "Israel," to the exclu-sion of the people who were indeed called "Israel" in the past, but she has in fact forfeited that title. Classic Christian theology is by and large based upon the assumption that the Church constitutes a new People, an "Israel of the Spirit." Interestingly enough, however, such an expression is absent from the New Testament, and Gutbrod provides an illuminating commentary.[17] First, in the synoptic Gospels, "Israel" never designates the Church. In the Gospel according to John, the term is used in a similar way as by the rabbis and is never extended to cover a "new Israel."[18] The book of Acts emphasizes the salvation of the Israel existing throughout all times.[19] In the epistles, "Israel" denotes the People of God. In Romans 11:26, the apostle exclaims: "all Israel will be saved" (not: all the *Jews*), but never is there a mention of a "new Israel."

Though Romans 9:6 states that "not all who are descended from Israel belong to Israel," this does not imply that Gentiles might legitimately be called "the true Israel" in replacement of a "false Israel." Romans 2:28–29 has already made it clear that there are two kinds of Jews, the outward and the inward; only the latter, says Paul, belong to *"verus Israel."*

True, there are texts like 1 Corinthians 10:18 where Paul speaks in a pejorative sense of an Israel *kata sarka* (according to the flesh). But here again, the intention is not to reject Israel as belonging to a debased realm of the flesh as opposed to the realm of immaterial spirit. Paul speaks here of the "outward"; he addresses himself to the morphological Israel without judgment of value, as when he was speaking of his correspondents of whom "not many are wise according to the flesh" (the RSV translates correctly: "according to worldly standards"), 1 Corinthians 1:26.

Moreover, the expression Israel *kata pneuma* (according to the Spirit) does *not* appear in the New Testament. This is no accident, for, in point of fact, such a concept is impossible in the perspective of Romans 11:17ff. The Gentiles have been grafted as "a wild olive shoot" on the olive tree (Rom. 11:16; cf. 11:1). There are, therefore, not two "Israels," one "after the flesh" and another one "after the spirit"; there is only the Israel of history to which Gentiles have been adjoined.[20]

Only one passage of the epistles can offer another understanding of the word "Israel." Galatians 6:16 (my translation) says: "Peace and mercy be upon all who conform themselves to this standard, so as upon the Israel of God."[21] The problem arises especially when the Greek text is translated in a leading way, as it often is. When read as it should be, it is clear that Paul, writing this passage with his own hand (Gal. 6:11), uses here a well-known Jewish literary device called *perat u-khelal* (from the particular to the general, Hillel's rule number 5 for exegesis); itself akin to the so-called *kal va-homer* (*a fortiori* argument, Hillel's rule number 1). So, peace and mercy be upon the Gentile Galatians who conform themselves to the apostolic teaching, and *a fortiori* and in general, upon the inclusive "Israel of God." The Synagogal prayer *Shemone esre* says in a similar manner:[22] "Grant, O our Father, peace, happiness, benediction, grace, mercy, compassion, to us and to the whole of Israel."

The categories used by St. Augustine to the effect of distinguishing between the visible and the invisible Church may be ecclesiologically questionable; it remains that we have here a fifth-century C.E. attempt to explicate a point of the Scriptures and the Jewish tradition. There has always been an "Israel" which, strictly speaking, bears that glorious name only because of the merits of the patriarchs, or thanks to the " 'seven thousand in Israel, all the knees that have not bowed to Baal, and every mouth that has not kissed him.' " (1 Kings 19:18; Rom. 11:4) These latter do not constitute a "spiritual Israel," a new People of God in replacement of the old unfaithful one. The admonitions of Elijah the prophet, and the famine he brings upon the land, are not addressed exclusively to some and not to others, but to all equally. It is also to all equally that the benediction of " 'a sound of the rushing of rain' " (1 Kings 18:41) is granted. When imposed on the Pauline demonstration, the Neoplatonic scheme of an ideal Israel opposed to a carnal one negates the very substance of the non-dualistic Hebraic and Biblical thinking.[23]

Israel is one. Gentiles have been associated with that one Israel, thus inaugurating the "end." The eschatological moment is reached because Israel's vocation of giving, and the pagans' vocation of receiving, *are* fulfilled. As we said above, this accomplishment is *already* present, but *not yet* lived up to because we are unwilling to assume the eschaton. This much is also true for the rabbinic concept of the kingdom of God. For the rabbis, the kingdom is already present in this world and some people actualize its potency in their own lives. David Flusser, quoting *Pirkē Aboth* 3:6, concludes: "There are individuals, therefore, who are already in the kingdom of heaven."[24] Flusser cites Leonhard Ragaz with approval: " 'It is not the eschatological expectation which determines Jesus' understanding of God and man . . . but, conversely, his understanding of God and man which determines his eschatological expectation.' "[25] This, to be sure, is very important. It makes clear that Jesus did not look at reality from a peculiar point of view he would forcibly apply to resisting phenomena. In other words, Jesus was no apocalypticist persuaded of the end of time in his own days and drawing from such a conviction the rest of his doctrine. Quite the other way around, his personal intimacy with God induced him to proclaim, in a genuine way, the proximity of the kingdom of God. To quote Flusser again: "He [Jesus] is the only Jew of ancient times known to us, who preached not only that men were on the threshold of the end of time, but that the new age of salvation had already begun."[26] History seems to have given at least one patent confirmation of this "good news." For it now happens that non-Jews are, with Jews, citizens of the kingdom of God; that they bring the divine kingdom to earth; that they minister to the world the reconciliation of all people to God (cf. 2 Cor. 5:18). Thus the prophecies are fulfilled which announced that "in the latter days . . . many peoples shall come and say: 'Come, let us go to the mountain of the Lord, to the house of the God of Jacob; that he may teach us in his ways and that we may walk in his paths. For out of Zion shall go forth the Torah, and the word of the Lord from Jerusalem.' " (Isa. 2:2–4, my translation)

From such a perspective, Paul is right in claiming the unity of Jews and Greeks before God, as of men and women, of free

men and slaves. This is a fact, however, which does not preclude
that as long as Paul lives the Christian communities among the
Gentiles acknowledge the primacy of Jerusalem. They make a
"contribution for the saints" of Jerusalem (cf. 1 Cor. 16:1–2; Acts
11:29; 24:17; 2 Cor. 8:1–9). Paul himself reports to the Twelve
"lest somehow I should be running or had run in vain." (Gal.
2:2)

Indeed, there were not two principles opposed in inescapable dualism which Christ solved by cutting the Gordian knot
of their incompatibility. On the contrary, ever since the beginning, *Israel* is the name given to the transcendence of all nations. That is why there is no Israel independent of the Gentiles.
Israel is the name of a promise, the promise that the slave is
destined to become free, the barbarian to become civilized, the
"wall of separation" to be abolished. Since the beginning, a
nation among others could be called "Israel" as a sign to all of
their eschaton. It was never an achieved static reality.

In a theological sense therefore it can be said that, with the
Nazarene event, *Israel* has crossed her boundaries and has
transformed all creation into herself; she has absorbed all that
had remained foreign to herself. This does not run contrary to
what we saw in chapter 7—that no pole of the two in mutual
presence is to absorb the other.

The question here is not one of confusion but of communion.
But once the nations and the Jewish people worship together
in Zion, according to their respective vocations, those "who
were once estranged" have become, with the Jews nothing else
but *Israel,* or, if we adopt the Augustinian formula, *"verus Israel."*

To remain within this limit established for our salvation is to
realize that the Gentiles are no longer without root and sap.
They have an age-old tree which bears and nourishes them.
They have a spiritual tutor, a guide in piety, in faith, and in
wisdom. They have a master: all Israel present in her Christ, in
her Holy Scriptures, in her tradition, in her apostolic witness,
in her history of salvation which continues even to the end of
time. All that is Israel; for Israel is one even as her God is one.

As the energy of God, she manifests God, all that is God, all that God wills, all that God gives—and that is God himself. God and Israel are married; they are inseparably united for eternity, "to the ages of ages." The covenant is indeed that serious: if the one is wounded, the Other is also; if one is estranged, the Other is also; if one is dead, the Other dies.[27]

The Gentile Christians have entered into that very covenant by adoption. There is no other covenant. Could God have bound himself more strongly than he has done since the beginning? Nothing has ever been missing in the relationship God-Israel. The expectation was simply that through the ultimate and fulfilled response of Israel to her God, this perfect commerce between them would be extended to the whole of creation. The "good tidings" of the Jewish disciples of the Nazarene are about the accomplishment of that agelong hope.

The "nations" have come to Zion, they have become integrated to Israel. Grafted onto the pure olive tree, they constitute the presence of the eschatological fulfillment of Israel. Truly and indeed, Israel has become "a light to the nations, she has opened the blind eyes and brought out the prisoners from the dungeon and those that sat in darkness out of the prison-house." (Isa. 42:6–7, my translation) So also Melchizedek before Abraham was the presence of Israel's future (cf. chapter 5 above). Similarly, the role of the Gentiles in the Church is to remind Israel of what she *is*. Not, to be sure, that the Church *qua* Church would provide an enviable perfection to the Synagogue, but, being "the Christ continued" (Bossuet), the Church —how unfaithfully indeed!—presents to the Jews and their real, positive, effective, holy dedication to God the image of their ultimate reference in the dedication of the Central Jew. As Juda Halevi puts it: "On the unique tree which is constituted by the history of salvation, Christianity is to Judaism that which branches, leaves and flowers are to the root."[28]

It may appear illusory and utopian to speak about the unity of Synagogue and Church and to "forget" about the centuries of persecutions and pogroms. Can an element exist capable of transcending even the murder of "Abel" by "Cain"? Despite the crime of the latter, are they still brothers? Is the Jewish author of Genesis 4:9 right in making God address Cain with the words: " 'Where is Abel your *brother?*' " And is Cain merely cynical in answering: " 'I do not know; am I *my brother's* keeper?' " What is that "mark [put] on Cain, lest any who came upon him should kill him"?

A study of the relationship envisaged by the Hebrew Scriptures between the Jew and the non-Jew resident in Israel will indicate a direction for our research.[29] This topic is relevant here because, just as Cain and Abel are separated by a murder, the Israelites and the *gerim* (resident aliens) are totally estranged from each other but are nonetheless brought, sometimes against their own will, in contact with each other. Then these two entities that everything seems to set apart are called to transcend their differences and become "brothers." The pragmatic necessity of coexistence plays here only a minor role; other groups of foreigners lived in Israel without being integrated and without constituting a challenge for the Jews. But not so the *gerim*. They brought within themselves an internal element to which Israel could not remain indifferent. Something as powerful as blood ties was able to create with the *gerim* a spiritual communion and a thrust towards a common destiny. This internal element is the non-possessing plight of the *gerim* which identifies them with widows, orphans, and the poor in Israel, so that the laws for the protection of the latter are also applicable to the former (cf. e. g., Deut. 14:29). Moreover, Israel confronted with the *ger* in her midst must remember that she has herself been *ger* (or *ebed*) in foreign lands (cf. Exod. 22:20; 23:9; Deut. 24:18, 22; 5:14–15). Both the Jew and the *ger* therefore are fundamentally participating in a common event, in a common destiny. The very deprivation, poverty, peregrinity of the *ger* is participation in Israel's history. It is thus understandable that the Israelites are called to love the *gerim* as themselves (Lev. 19:34; Deut. 10:19), for it really *is* a matter of themselves. These foreigners are a mirror of the Israelites' own soul. Like the Jews, they are under God's compassionate and jealous protection (Deut. 10:18; Mal. 3:5; Ps. 146:9). In the End, the *"gerim"* will be joint-heirs of the holy land (Ezek. 47:22).

Of course, there is a status of *gerim* which needs to be fulfilled by the non-Jews in the first place.[30] Then only may the "aliens" claim the protection of the Torah and the acknowledgment by the Synagogue of the existential unity which binds it and them together. That is why 1 Peter 2:11 says to Christians that they are strangers and pilgrims on the earth (a declaration of identity with which the Christians of this country in particular are called to compare their present status). For, in the measure that Gentiles have chosen to partake in Israel's destiny, " 'God, who knows the heart, bore witness to them, giving them the Holy Spirit just as he did to us [Jews]; and he made no distinction between us [Jews] and them, but cleansed their hearts by faith.' " (Acts 15:8–9) These words of Peter at the first council of Jerusalem are uttered on behalf of Gentiles who entered the People of God. What finally proved decisive in the debate between those who taught that " 'Unless you are circumcised according to the custom of Moses, you cannot be saved,' " on the one hand, and Paul and Barnabas, on the other, was all the "signs and wonders God had done . . . among the Gentiles" showing that " 'God first visited the Gentiles, to take out of them a people for his name. And with this the words of the prophets agree.' " (Acts 15:1, 12, 14)

"Cain" is reconciled with "Abel." Both are again the brothers they never ceased to be. " 'We, the apostles and the elders [of Israel], your brothers, send greetings to all our brothers of Gentile birth who live in Antioch, Syria, and Cilicia.' " (Acts 15:23, TEV) Only Abel, here represented by the apostles and elders of Israel, can call Cain "brother." In the synod of Jerusalem, according to Acts 15, the Gentiles themselves were significantly absent. The discussion took place between Jews. *Gentiles have nothing to say because they have nothing to forgive.* Only Jews can and may give a positive meaning to Esau's kiss (Gen. 33:4). According to rabbinic tradition, the dots which are placed over the letters of the Hebrew word "and he kissed him" either

indicate the duplicity of Esau, or they "lie" and Esau's kiss was
a real kiss of peace. This ambiguity can only be solved and
removed by Jacob's forgiveness.[31]

Some thirty-five years have elapsed since Auschwitz. An
incredible number of changes have transformed our universe
and, among other constituting elements, Judaism and Christianity. These two find themselves having at least one thing in
common: they are under the threat of annihilation. Nobody
knows if tomorrow there will still be something like Judaism, or
like Christianity, or whether the human race itself will survive.

As Jews or Christians, as human beings involved in a danger-
ous world, we feel both *impotent* and ultimately responsible.
We are conscious of being manipulated by forces we do not
control, but of being nonetheless the human soul of the immense machine which both enhances our well-being and
crushes us and our children. Tomorrow is the great unknown,
and beyond our reach, especially if by this we mean that we are
unable to shape a tomorrow in the resemblance of our dream,
in the likeness of the fancied representation of our imagination.
But tomorrow will be what we make of our today: Judaism
tomorrow and Christianity tomorrow will look like our own
soul, they will mirror our inner selves. If the image they reflect
is monstrous, it will be because Jews and Christians have become monsters. If the image is redeemed and conforms to the
likeness of "one like a son of man" (Dan. 7:13), it will be because
we shall have retrieved our true human identity.

As far as the relationship between Synagogue and Church is
concerned, the question is not whether Jews and Christians can
"better" relate to each other and contrive a formula of "peaceful coexistence." For Auschwitz is the outcome of such a *modus
vivendi!* What we can hope the formidable mutations of our
universe will yield goes much beyond the retrieval of the nine-
teenth-century civility between Judaism and Christianity. What
then will the relationship be? This is a question which cannot

be answered with any degree of certainty, for what is in store *has in fact no precedent in history.* We can, however, venture some prognosis.

First let me add a few enlightening points to the historical background I have evoked so far and against which the Jewish-Christian relationship takes place. Contrary to a common cliché, the schism in Judaism between two trends, the one of messianic expectations, the other of legalistic conceptions, must be traced back beyond the beginning of the Christian era. The bifurcation between so-called classical or rabbinic Judaism, on the one hand, and apocalyptic, millennium-minded Judaism, on the other, is to be situated *before* the birth of Christianity which only later belonged to this non-orthodox branch. Apocalyptic Judaism adopted a path of its own which had *practical* consequences that the "Sages, their memory be blessed," felt it impossible to condone; but ideologically it was not and could not be simply excommunicated.[32] By non-classical Judaism, I mean historical movements such as Hellenistic Judaism, Qumran, Essenism, Hasidism (of the Rhineland and, later, of Eastern Europe), the diverse aspects of Jewish mysticism, Zealotism, Christianity—of course all these "left wing" expressions of Judaism are not to be confused. My point is that they have grown on a common soil and shared in a common genius, a genius which Judaism, and even rabbinic Judaism simply could not and still cannot afford to ignore.

What about Christianity?

We have seen above that, in conformity with so many other spiritual movements—for instance, Hasidism—the original Christian fervor and purity was short-lived. The amazingly swift penetration of Christianity into the Hellenistic world was accompanied by a terrible attrition of substance. Becoming fashionable, Christianity adopted a Greek mind-set in many ways foreign to the Jewish message. The divorce from the Synagogue soon became irreparable and, instead of being alarmed by such a disastrous situation, the Gentile Church made virtue of necessity. The ordeal, the traumatic crisis, through which many Christians pass today, especially Roman Catholics, reveals how deeply rooted the weeds of Hellenistic dualism and idealism were.

On the other hand, we witness fascinating attempts on the part of Jewish scholars to reappraise the person and message of the Nazarene and the religious persuasions of the primitive Church. In so doing, no matter what amount of empathy is involved in the research, Jewish critics necessarily bump into the obstacle of the Christian conception of the Law. This issue, especially as proposed by Paul, is an inevitable block on the road to an encounter with Jesus or his disciples.

But, as I have pointed out above (chapter 6), Paul saw in Jesus the possibility at last fully given to us of a total and limitless relationship with God, a relationship in which law-abiding meant ultimately the total sacrifice of (this Central One of) ourselves before God. What Paul did not realize, however, was that his impassioned plea would sometimes be taken out of context. What was originally said *inside* the framework provided by the Torah granted to Israel would at some time be considered by Gentiles as an attack launched by an outsider against the Law and Judaism. What in Paul's mind was the ultimate possibility for the Torah to be fulfilled became—for 2000 years of irrecoverable twisting of historical truth—a complete rejection by the Jew Paul of his Judaism and Jewishness. True, twenty centuries of history are a heavy load to carry, but we must today realize that there is no justification whatsoever in adopting a non-Jewish and anti-Semitic view about Paul. On the contrary, a true encounter with him would purge the Church of the poisonous drugs mixed in her blood. Paul has something to tell today's Church which would bring her to repentance for her insatiable thirst for power and for being at the first place in God's heart at the expense of the chosen people (cf. Rom. 9—11; Eph. 2).

The terrible convulsions of the twentieth century are the tortured expression of its quest for authenticity. After a time which looks like an eternity during which people and their institutions were content with carrying the mask of a fake identity, the apocalyptic moment of truth has come. For Christians, it means the painful birthing of none other than Christ. There is for the Church the possibility of a resurrection in the valley of judgment. If she bypasses this last chance, however, her bones will know the expected natural decay and be reduced to dust.

As for the Synagogue, on the other hand, Richard Rubenstein is perhaps right in claiming that Paul the Jew has something to say to his fellow Jews on the question of how to fulfill the Torah.[33] More than that, perhaps the time has come for going beyond the historical divisions between the "Establishments" called Judaism and Christianity. Perhaps the healing of the wounds inflicted by the war between the generations must start at the root of that war, between mother and daughter, father and son, Synagogue and Church. Perhaps the time has come for going BEYOND JUDAISM AND CHRISTIANITY *QUA* INSTITUTIONS!

I realize the gravity of my statement. Until the dark bloody years of the Third Reich, such an idea would have been inconceivable or, at least, irresponsible. But since those days we have lived together the horror of Auschwitz in which a pretendedly "Christianized" world tried to annihilate, in the paroxysm of a black mass, its (Jewish, and thus divine) genitor. After Auschwitz, nothing can be as before. In more than one way, the time since Auschwitz resembles the time after Golgotha: we live in a new era and we *must*, as Paul did in his day, draw the necessary conclusion of the newness of our time: "a new world is in place; the old one is gone, and a new order has begun." (2 Cor. 5:17, my translation)

In what way this time is a new time, this order a new order, in fact depends upon our willingness to accept its newness. In this respect, as in any other, the "given" remains a dead letter as long as we do not grant it life.[34] The "new" is a renewed possibility, a renewed covenant between God and humanity, a curve in the dialogue between him and us. Now, what shall we

say? What content shall we put in the cup offered? What kind
of partner will God encounter in us? What sort of personality
will he find in his embrace? The question remains open, as
when Jacob and Esau kissed each other at Penuel (Gen. 33:4, cf.
above). By this I do not mean anything theoretical, not even
mystical, for the relationship with God is essentially what our
relationship with our neighbor is. The problem is historical; it
is existential; tomorrow flows from our today. It is today that the
chance is given to us to redeem ourselves, to save the world, to
encounter the other in whose person we are invited to discover
the Shekinah, the divine presence. If our time has taught us
something about ourselves and about our world, it is that we are
all one, and that humanity is one. We do know by now that we
shall perish together or live together. All provincialism, particularism, racism, nationalism, isolationism is irremediably outdated. Today, we know that "Jewish" or "Christian" problems
go overboard; they are *human* problems. True, they always
have been. The difference is that today, hopefully, we discover
that *verus Israel* and *verus populus Christianus* have in common a genuine approach to those problems. Not only is the fiery
furnace the same for the one and the other, but so is the interpretation of it and the salvation from it (or *in* it). To pick a
random example, it is clear that the "drug culture" corresponds
to a deep feeling of despair among our contemporaries, a despair that neither Judaism nor Christianity has been able to
prevent. The phenomenon cannot, it may not be faced by Jews
merely for the sake of Jews, or by Christians merely for the sake
of Christians. In both Church and Synagogue, the plague has
similar spiritual causes, ranging from incapacity to speak a
human modern language in communicating with the new generation to the spectacle of a sclerotic Establishment usurping
the title of Judaic or Christian. It also has similar effects which
are felt in both instances on the existential level of the fundamental choice between commitment and alienation. Drug
abuse, the catastrophic failure of the "institution of marriage"
in our society, the wave of abortions, the rapidly widening erup-
tion of a demonic "spiritualism" in this country—all call for a

reappraisal of our Judeo-Christian heritage, of our common world view, of our conception of society, of our understanding of God. It is only in a common research wrought by a common will that, together, we may hope to be able to address ourselves to these problems and to all of humanity's problems.

What is certain is that no miracle will ever happen if the groups turn in upon themselves and exclude the others. It is not enough that Jews rediscover their brotherhood and Christians theirs. God is not the God of scattered groups but the Lord of us all. Sooner or later—O Church, O Synagogue—we will have to face each other, like Jacob and Esau. It is only at the meeting place that the angel is waiting for us; there is Penuel, the face of God, God's presence.

In this book I have addressed myself much more to the necessity for the Church to reestablish her communion with the Synagogue than to the desirability for the latter to have a love affair of sorts with the Church. Let me here balance my argument in reflecting upon what the Synagogue might "gain" from opening herself to her transfiguration into the Israel where there are neither Greeks nor Jews.

I have already quoted Richard Rubenstein in what precedes. Rubenstein psychoanalyzes the Biblical message of Israel and, in a way, dismantles piece by piece the stronghold of a dogmatic, arrogant castle. His conclusion is well known: he rejects Judeo-Christianity and advocates a return to paganism as a more honest response to the human predicament. Auschwitz has demonstrated once and for all that God, the God of Judeo-Christianity, is not the Lord of history. And if God is not omnipotent, he is "useless"!

Rubenstein's analysis, however, can in its turn be psychoanalyzed. His inability, or his refusal, to see any kind of meaning in Auschwitz or in the death of an infant expresses his inability to integrate failure. Rubenstein repeats about Auschwitz, insofar as he is concerned, what has been so often true for so many Jews about the cross of Calvary: he negates any meaningfulness in the event, lest God be dead. Rubenstein's mistake—a typical mistake indeed—is to interpret Judeo-Christianity as in quest of

omnipotence in the image of an omnipotent God. Both terms
of Rubenstein's statement are questionable. First of all, God's
omnipotence is an expression of faith, not a mathematical
axiom; and second, the God of Israel certainly does not promise
omnipotence to his people, but hardship. "But Joshua said to
the people, 'You cannot serve the LORD; for he is a holy God;
he is a jealous God; he will not forgive your transgressions or
your sins. If you forsake the LORD and serve foreign gods, then
he will turn and do you harm, and consume you, after having
done you good.'" (Josh. 24:19–20)

Far from luring us with the promise that we will be granted
power, God calls us to give up appetite for power; we are free
to *become* only when we muzzle our greediness to *have*. The
"having" enslaves us; only the one who has nothing to lose can
at last be preoccupied with something more important than the
static protection of static riches. In these possessions there is no
other soul but the one they have stolen from their "owner."

This, I trust, is the core of the Christian message. To God's
kenosis (emptiness, Phil. 2:7), to God's *"tsimtsum"* (shrinkage,
Zohar), for our sake, must correspond our stripping of all pre-
tense before his face. It means that:

—No effort to fulfill the Law will ever suffice to gain us a
positive balance-sheet when confronting the Judge.

—No effort will ever succeed in placating the righteous
wrath of the Great Demander. ("You shall not have the
strength," said Joshua.)

—No effort will ever suffice to appease the righteous jealousy
of the Great Impassionate.[35]

—No effort will ever suffice to make us measure up to the
devouring love of the Great Lover.

Is there any reason then for keeping the commandments? In
all honesty and frankness: NONE! Unless one calls love and
gratuitousness reason. This is the central theme of the book of
Job. "'Does Job fear God for nought?'" is the innuendo of Satan
(1:9); and the whole book is a demonstration that the relationship between God and Job is *"le-ḥinnam"* (without gain, for
nought, without logical justification). "'Be good disciples,'" says

Pirkē Aboth 1:3, " 'serving their master without expectation of reward.' "

The Jews who constituted the primitive Christian community had the genius to proclaim that in the death of an innocent man on the altar of the offering to God lay the ultimate human response to God's love. Beyond this no one can go. But, less than this, one can always do something more for the love of God—and there is no fulfillment.

Is this a message possible to accept today? Are we going to thrust together beyond the institutions of Judaism and Christianity? Perhaps I am dreaming, perhaps all this is the fruit of my imagination impatient to leap into the kingdom of God . . . and I remember that for Franz Kafka impatience is the gravest of all sins. But one thing remains forever true: it is up to us to choose good and life in order to live.

Now it may be that to live means, for the time to come, to live in the separation between Mother and Daughter, between Priest and Laity, between the source of living waters and those who must drink therefrom, between the light and the nations.

As for me and my house—as Joshua said—
we raise the Hillelite question: *"im lo
'akhshayw eymathay?"*—"if not now, then when?"

Notes

Chapter 1. THE IDENTITY OF ISRAEL

1. Émile M. Cioran, *La Tentation d'exister* (Paris: Gallimard, 1956), p. 82 (my translation).
2. Rudolf Bultmann, *Jesus Christ and Mythology* (New York: Charles Scribner's Sons, 1958), p. 49.
3. See Albrecht Alt, *Essays on Old Testament History and Religion,* trans. R. A. Wilson (Garden City, N.Y.: Doubleday, 1967).
4. Cf. Julian Morgenstern, *The Book of Genesis* (1919; reprint ed., New York: Schocken Books, 1965), p. 8:

    the non-Jewish scholars . . . have failed in considerable measure to determine the ends for which these sources were combined and the thoughts and aims which animated the editors. . . . they have failed to realize and to stress that the Old Testament . . . is entirely a Jewish work, written by Jewish authors and edited by Jewish thinkers, the product of Jewish religious genius and a unit of Jewish thought and doctrine, and that it must be animated throughout by some deeply Jewish purpose, and can, in the final analysis, be correctly understood only when interpreted from a positive Jewish standpoint.

Chapter 2. GOD'S PRIVATE PROPERTY

1. Jean-Paul Sartre, *The Flies* (New York: Vintage Book, 1947), act 2, scene 2.
2. See chapter 4 below, "The Holy Nation."
3. Or (as Hebrew conception is refractory to such an abstract concept as "nothingness"), God has created the universe from "the nonliving," from a corpse, a chaos. The same idea appears in Ezekiel 37.
4. Gerhard von Rad, *Genesis: A Commentary,* trans. John H. Marks (Philadelphia: The Westminster Press, 1961), cf. p. 44.
5. In the Greek of the New Testament, the term is *(ap)arche* or *prototokos.*
6. Such a dramatic dimension is conveyed by (among other texts) the debate God has with himself before raising up man. " 'Let *us* make man in *our* own image.' " (Gen. 1:26, my italics) The plural

in the sentence is unexpected. It has puzzled exegetes for centuries. Without rejecting the possibility that God may have spoken to himself, or to his angels, or to the world so far in existence, the Jewish tradition, interestingly enough, intimates that God in fact spoke to the man himself, to the soon-to-be Adam whose birth can only be the blessed fruit of the marriage between the Creator and the man himself, paradoxically as it may appear. (But cf. Job 38ff.) For Adam here is understood as a continuous project of God's will, as a continuous fulfillment of human dedication. Man—humanity —is a gerundive (something in thrust towards its achievement).

7. "Moses looked this way and that," says Exodus 2:12 (my translation), "and he saw *no one.*" Cf. Isaiah 60:16; Job 38:4–6.

8. Taking into account the fact that all Hebrew manuscripts of Genesis 2:4 present the anomaly that one of the consonants is written smaller than the others in the word *"lehibbar'am"* ("when they were created"), the rabbis conclude that the text can also be read through alliteration as *"le'abraham"!* It is "for Abraham" that the heavens and the earth have been called into existence.

9. Exodus 12:38: "A mixed multitude also went up with them"; cf. Numbers 11:14.

10. Cf. Leviticus 19:10, 33, 34; 23:22; Numbers 9:14; 15:14ff.; 35:15; Deuteronomy 14:29, etc.

11. Morton Smith, *Palestinian Parties and Politics That Shaped the Old Testament* (New York: Columbia University Press, 1971).

12. The Levites' "alien-ness" is the mirror of one of the main features of the Hebrew people at large. As Gerhard von Rad writes (*Genesis: A Commentary,* p. 154), "Taken from the community of nations (cf. Num. 23.9) and never truly rooted in Canaan, but even there a stranger (cf. Lev. 25.23; Ps. 39.12), Israel saw herself being led on a special road whose plan and goal lay completely in Yahweh's hand."

13. The Zohar (V.221*b*) comments: "God has made Israel as it were the heart of all mankind, and as the limbs cannot endure for a moment without the heart, so the other nations cannot endure without Israel." *The Zohar,* trans. Maurice Simon and Harry Sperling, 5 vols. (London: The Soncino Press, 1949), V:331.

14. Wishing *shalom* to somebody is uttering the wish that that person be "whole," be in possession of all the faculties which God bestows and which enable us to turn freely and totally toward God in dialogue with him. To offer *shalom* requires the spirit of invention which fills all emptiness.

Chapter 3. THE KINGDOM OF PRIESTS

1. Cf. Deuteronomy 27:9; Joshua 24. For some modern views on this, see George E. Mendenhall, *Law and Covenant in Israel and the Ancient Near East* (Pittsburgh: Biblical Colloquium, 1955); Klaus Baltzer, *Das Bundesformular*, Wissenschaftliche Monographien zum Alten und Neuen Testament (Neukirchen: Neukirchener Verlag, 1960); English translation: *The Covenant Formulary: In Old Testament, Jewish, and Early Christian Writings*, trans. David E. Green (Philadelphia: Fortress Press, 1971); Dennis J. McCarthy, *Treaty and Covenant: A Study in Form in the Ancient Oriental Documents and the Old Testament* (Rome: Pontifical Biblical Institute, 1963); idem, *Old Testament Covenant: A Survey of Current Opinions* (Richmond: John Knox Press, 1972).

2. Gerhard von Rad, *The Problem of the Hexateuch and Other Essays* (New York: McGraw-Hill, 1966), p. 40.

3. Martin Noth, *Überlieferungsgeschichte des Pentateuch* (Stuttgart: Kohlhammer, 1948); idem, *Das System der zwölf Stämme Israels*, Beiträge zur Wissenschaft vom Alten und Neuen Testament (Stuttgart: Kohlhammer, 1930; reprint ed., Darmstadt: Wissenschaftliche Buchgesellschaft, 1966), p. 121.

4. Hans Wildberger, *Jahwes Eigentumsvolk* (Zurich: Zwingli Verlag, 1960).

5. All this nevertheless seems insufficient evidence to posit a deuteronomic authorship for Exodus 19. *Goy qodesh*, for instance, appears to be in contrast with the use of *'am* (people) in Deuteronomy (cf. 7:6; 14:2, 21; 26:19; 28:9). Note that the combination of *'am* with *qodesh* is also found in Isaiah 62:12 and Jeremiah 2:3. The situation is further complicated by the expression *beith Yaaqob* (house of Jacob) in Exodus 19:3 which seems to be a later element in the text, the first datable usage of which is in Amos 3:13, imitated later by Isaiah, Micah, Second Isaiah, Jeremiah, and Obadiah. The same judgment applies to the perhaps non-genuine conditional clause stressing obedience to the commandments as a condition for the fulfillment of the promise. For Martin Buber this is a late gloss. Gerhard von Rad, in his turn, rejects the deuteronomistic filiation of our text.

It seems that before being inserted into the context of the Sinai covenant, Exodus 19:4–6 was in use during the first decades of Israel's kingdom, at a time when the festival of Succoth, or (according to Hans Wildberger) the festival of Matsoth, was still in force in Shechem or Gilgal. Such in any case is the opinion of Sigmund Mowinckel. See his *Le Décalogue* (Paris: Félix Alcan, 1927), pp. 128ff. Mowinckel directs attention to the mixture of prophetic and exhortative elements in Exodus 19. Such a genre (also exemplified in Pss. 50; 81; 95) belongs, he says, within the framework of the New Year festival, combined with Succoth, the main features of these cultic prophecies being the call to remain faithful to the covenant, and acknowledgments of the kingship of Yhwh.

6. Cf. Emmanuel Podechard, *Le Psautier II* (Lyon: Faculté catholique de Lyon, 1954); Elmer A. Leslie, *The Psalms* (Nashville: Abingdon-Cokesbury, 1949), p. 103. Psalm 114:2 is a more remote parallel. There are also parallel motifs in Exodus 15:17–18. Cf. Numbers 11:29 (the whole nation is prophetic) and Hosea 4:6 (the whole nation is priestly).

7. Cf. Wilhelm Caspari, "Das priesterliche Königreich," *Theologische Blätter* 8 (1929):106–110; Mark Lidzbarski, *Altsemitische Texte* (Giessen: Alfred Töpelmann, 1907), vol. 1, pp. 12ff. On the other side, Hans Wildberger, *Jahwes Eigentumsvolk,* p. 80 notices that *mamlekheth* never has the meaning "king" in the Scriptures.

8. David, for instance, did not see priestly functions as totally alien to his royal office. It was he who was responsible for carrying the ark to Jerusalem. He dressed like a priest (2 Sam. 6:14; 1 Chron. 15:27), and, again like a priest, he sacrificed and danced before the ark (2 Sam. 6:13, 16). He blessed his family (1 Chron. 16:43); he intended to build the Temple (in fact, a royal chapel); and, according to a persistent tradition, he created the pattern for divine worship. David is, moreover, traditionally the author of many Psalms. The priests Zadok and Abiathar owed their appointments to him, and even his sons were appointed *kohanim* (priests) by him in 2 Samuel 8:18! (Cf. 20:26; 1 Kings 4:5; 1 Chron. 18:17.)

   Was David, then, also a priest? Psalm 110 suggests that the two aspects—kingship and priesthood—were combined during the period of the unified monarchy.

9. Martin Buber, *Moses* (New York: Harper and Brothers, 1948), p. 119. Cf. Isaiah 61:6 (written ca. 537-515). James Muilenburg, "Exegesis" for the Book of Isaiah, *The Interpreter's Bible,* 12 vols. (New York: Abingdon, 1956), 5:712 writes: "Zion's unique status will be recognized; among the peoples of the world she will serve as *priests* just as the Aaronids did in Israel (cf. Exod. 19:6; I Pet. 2:9); she will perform the priestly functions of instruction and intercession (cf. 45:14–15; 60:14; also 66:21)."

   By the second century B.C.E., however, the expression was understood as "a kingdom and priests"; cf. Ethiopic Jubilees 16:18 [the original was written around 150–100 B.C.E.; R. H. Charles sees this text in Ethiopic as faithful to the Hebrew original]; 2 Maccabees 2:18 [ca. 124 B.C.E.]; Philo, *De Abrahamo* 56; idem, *De Sobrietate* 66. The Targums on Exodus 19:6 saw an accumulation of three privileges granted to Israel. They are "kings and priests, and a holy nation"; cf. Neofiti; Frag. Tg; Cairo Geniza ms. F; the situation is the same in Ps. Jon.; Onk.; and Peshitta. Cf. Revelation 1:5–6; 5:9–10.

One can summarize the different options as the following: (a) a kingdom composed of priests (cf. book of Revelations); (b) a kingdom with a collective priestly responsibility on behalf of all peoples (cf. E. L. Ehrlich and A. H. McNeile); (c) a hierocracy (a kingdom ruled by priests; cf. the high priest Joshua receiving the crown in Zech. 6:11); and (d) "a kingdom set apart like a priesthood and possessing collectively the priestly status of a holy nation," in the words of R. B. Y. Scott.

10. Cf., for example, Norman Snaith, *The Distinctive Ideas of the Old Testament* (Philadelphia: The Westminster Press, 1946), pp. 24ff., his chapter on "holiness."

11. On this matter, see Sigmund Mowinckel, *Psalmenstudien* (Oslo, 1921–24; reprint ed., Amsterdam: Verlag P. Schippers, 1961); Martin Buber, *The Kingship of God,* trans. Richard Scheimann (New York: Harper & Row, 1967); Jean de Fraine, *L'Aspect religieux de la royauté israélite* (Rome: Pontifical Biblical Institute, 1954). God's kingship is clearly expressed for the first time in Isaiah 6:5. But it appears as early as the episode of Balaam (Num. 23:21).

12. Cf. Martin Buber, *The Prophetic Faith,* trans. Carlyle Witton-Davies (New York: Harper & Row, 1960). In the original *(Torath ha-Nebiim),* p. 147.

13. Edmond Jacob, *Theology of the Old Testament,* trans. Arthur Heathcote and Philip J. Allcock (New York: Harper & Row, 1958), pp. 247, 249.

14. It is to be noticed that in the Scriptures property belongs integrally to the person, so that it sometimes is called *nephesh* ("soul"; Gen. 12:5). Property is the support of one's being.

15. It is referred to in nearly all the other books of Scripture. Cf. David Daube, *The Exodus Pattern in the Bible* (London: Faber and Faber, 1963).

16. Cf. Johannes Pedersen, *Israel, Its Life and Culture,* 4 vols. (London: Oxford University Press, 1940), III–IV:737: "Moses . . . has certain traits of the idealised king."

17. André Lacocque, "L'Idée directrice de Exode I à IV," *Vetus Testamentum* 15 (1965):345ff.; idem, *Le Devenir de Dieu* (Paris: Éditions universitaires, 1967), pp. 161ff.

18. The theme of substitution is quite obvious in the narratives on the Paschal lamb. Exodus 12 relates the "event"; Exodus 13 its "institution." In both cases, the sacrifice is bound up with the fate of the firstborn children, for the best as far as the Israelites are concerned, for the worst in regard to the Egyptians. This meets per-

fectly the Torah-principle according to which the firstborn belongs to God—like blood or life—and must therefore be rendered
to him (Num. 3:12, 41; 8:16–17). Israel as a whole is herself the
firstborn of God (Exod. 4:22; Jer. 31:9 [Ephraim]; Zech. 12:10; 1
Chron. 5:1). Israel is the "Prime," the offspring of the virile potency of the Father-God (cf. Gen. 49:3; Deut. 21:17). That is why
the death of the Egyptian firstborn is a ransom for the murder of
the Hebrew firstborn (Exod. 4:22–23; cf. 12:11ff. where the root
"pdh," to ransom, is to be noted; 22:23–24; Num. 3:13; 8:17, etc.).

19. See my *Le Devenir de Dieu,* pp. 49ff.
20. It is to be noted that the process of democratization of the priesthood was completed by the time Isaiah 61:4–11 was written (at
least in the eyes of the party of opposition in Jerusalem). Similarly,
in Isaiah 62:3 the royal symbols are applied to the whole nation.
Isaiah 61:4–11 implicitly universalizes prophecy as it assimilates
the prophetic with the priestly. On the latter point, see Joel 3;
Isaiah 32:15–17; Ezekiel 36:26–27.
21. *Urzeit* will find its response in *Endzeit.*
22. A striking example is provided by the mosaic-like 19th chapter of
Leviticus. On the eschatologically realized breaking down of all
distinction between sacred and profane, see Zechariah 14.
23. Cf. Numbers 4:15; Leviticus 7:21; 10:2; 1 Samuel 6:19; 2 Samuel
6:6–7; 24:1, 10, 15; 2 Kings 2:23–25; 23:9; 2 Chronicles 26:19.
24. See the following chapter (4).
25. Cf. Edmond Jacob, *Theology of the Old Testament,* p. 250.
26. This was at the heart of the protest in Qumran. The Jerusalem
priests had become unworthy—apostates in the judgment of the
sectarian community. Consequently, were it not for Qumran and
its true priesthood, Israel would no longer be Israel.
27. Cf. the Wisdom of Solomon 5:4–5: "[The ungodly shall say:] 'This
is the man whom we once held in derision and made a byword of
reproach—we fools! We thought that his life was madness and that
his end was without honor. Why has he been numbered among the
sons of God? And why is his lot among the saints?' "
28. See "Appendix to Chapter 3" at the end of this chapter.
29. According to a Jewish mystical tradition there are throughout the
generations 36 (numerical value of the Hebrew letters *lamed* and
vav) righteous men who save the world from catastrophe and
chaos.
30. Markus Barth, *Israel und die Kirche im Brief des Paulus an die
Epheser,* Theologische Existenz Heute 75 (Munich: Chr. Kaiser,
1959), pp. 38–39 (my translation): "Israel is *the* missionary chosen
by God among the heathens. This fact is not only valid for the
witness which Israel bears in words, but equally in that she must
become, by her own blessing, a blessing for all the nations. She

becomes through her punishment the example of all punishments; her gathering and reestablishment mean salvation for all the nations near and far." Again, "all nations owe to the election of Israel for divine service the knowledge of God's existence and essence. Because of the existence of Israel in their midst the nations cannot avoid the manifestation of God in space and in time. Thanks to the wrath and to the love of God upon his people and its representatives, the nations know that 'mercy triumphs over judgment.' (James 2:13) 'From Israel, in natural descent, sprang the Messiah.' (Rom. 9:5)"

31. Paul Ricoeur, *The Symbolism of Evil*, trans. Emerson Buchanan (New York: Harper & Row, 1967), p. 68. In the French original, p. 70. Emphasis mine.

32. *Ibid.*, p. 251.

33. Georg Hamann, *Schriften* (Berlin: G. Reimer, 1821), vol. 1, p. 450 (my translation).

34. That any "chair," for example, can be called "(God's) throne" in Hebrew is descriptive of what we may call the eschatological dimension of an object which ceases to be indifferent and passes into the plane of the I-Thou relationship. See chapter 4 for further elaboration.

35. Tennessee Williams, *Suddenly Last Summer* (New York: New Directions, 1958): "We are all children in a large kindergarten, trying to spell the Name of God with wrong alphabet blocks."

36. Cf. *Sanh.* 59a; *B.K.* 38a; *A.Z.* 3a; *Sifra Shemoth* 13 (ed. Weiss 86b).

37. Cf. *Shabb.* 10a; Zohar I.5a: "Man associates himself with God for the work of the Beginning."

38. Cf. the numerous texts with "for thy name's sake": Psalm 25:11; Daniel 9:9; also Psalm 79:9; Isaiah 43:25; Jeremiah 14:7, 21.

    The Midrash goes further (*Berak.* 59a): "When God remembers his children who dwell in misery among the nations of the world, he causes two tears to descend to the ocean and the sound is heard from one end of the world to the other." Again (*Pesikta* 166a, b and *Lam. R.*, Romm. 15a, col. 2): "When the Israelites do God's will, they add to the power of God on high. When the Israelites do not do God's will, they as it were weaken the great power of God on high."

    And (*Mid. Ps.*, Buber 255a; *Sifre*, Friedman 144a; *Pesikta* 102b): " 'Ye are my witnesses, saith the Lord, and I am God.' (Isa. 43:12 [KJV]) That is, when ye are my witnesses I am God, and when ye are not my witnesses I am as it were not God."

    Similarly (*Mid. Ps.*, Buber 255a; *Sifre*, Friedman 144a): " 'Unto thee I lift up mine eyes O thou that sittest in the heavens' . . . (Ps. 123:1). . . . If it were not for me, i. e., if I did not lift up my eyes, Thou O God wouldst not be sitting in the heavens."

39. Robert H. Pfeiffer, *Introduction to the Old Testament* (New York: Harper & Brothers, 1940), pp. 28–29.

40. Cf. Philo, *De Vita Mosis* I, 44; Acts 7:23–29; Hebrews 11:24–27. St. Augustine in *Contra Faustum* xxii, 70 wonders if Moses' act was legitimate, but in *Quaestiones in Heptateuchum* II, 2 he admits that Moses was divinely inspired in this respect.

41. André Neher, *Moses and the Vocation of the Jewish People*, trans. Irene Marinoff (New York: Harper Torchbook, 1959), p. 80.

Chapter 4. THE HOLY NATION

1. Cf. Psalms 23:4; 102:12; 144:4; Job 8:9; 14:2; Ecclesiasticus 6:12; 8:13; 1 Chronicles 29:15, etc. Cf. the Wisdom of Solomon 5:8–13:

   > "What has our arrogance profited us? And what good has our boasted wealth brought us? All those things have vanished like a shadow, and like a rumor that passes by; like a ship that sails through the billowy water, and when it has passed no trace can be found, nor track of its keel in the waves; or as, when a bird flies through the air, no evidence of its passage is found; the light air, lashed by the beat of its pinions . . . . So we also, as soon as we were born, ceased to be, and we had no sign of virtue to show, but were consumed in our wickedness."

2. Albert Camus, *La Peste* (Paris: Gallimard, 1947), pp. 302–304. English translation: *The Plague*, trans. Stuart Gilbert (New York: Alfred A. Knopf, 1960), pp. 229–231.

3. The fear and terror of failure, says Paul Ricoeur (*The Symbolism of Evil*, p. 27), result from a definition of defilement "in which the ethical order of doing ill has not been distinguished from the cosmo-biological order of faring ill: suffering, sickness, death, failure." Job had to pull himself out of that confusion. For the conception of a distributive chastisement "transforms all possible sufferings, all diseases, all death, all failure into a sign of defilement." In the French original, p. 33.

4. Cf. Claude Tresmontant, *Saint Paul and the Mystery of Christ*, trans. Donald Attwater (New York: Harper Torchbook, 1957), p. 82: "This dialectic of failure and success, of success in and through failure, is a constant element in Israel's history and in all biblical thought. It is to be found in Israel's very constitution." Cf. Deuteronomy 7:7; Isaiah 53; Judges 7:2; 1 Samuel 17:45.

5. André Neher, "L'Échec dans la perspective juive" in Jean Lacroix, *Les hommes devant l'échec* (Paris: Presses Universitaires de France, 1968), p. 148.

6. The fact that the record of Israel's slavery in Egypt received its final literary form in the tenth century B.C.E. as a means of accounting for the happy and settled circumstances of the Solomonic period does not change its factuality. There are many nations which also experienced leaving a "house of bondage." Amos is aware of this (9:7). But only Israel took pains, and indeed *pride*, not only in keeping a record of her slavery, but in repeating it as a leitmotiv in her judicial codes (cf. Deut. 5:15; 15:15; 16:12, etc.). For Martin Buber *(Moses, ad loc.)*, this fact is unparalleled in history.

7. Though the future tense is correct according to the Greek of the New Testament, one too often overlooks the present tense in the first part of the sentence in all the Beatitudes (" 'Blessed *are* . . .' "). Moreover, the first, the eighth, and the ninth continue in the present—supplementary evidence that syntactically these sentences have an unmistakably Hebrew or Aramaic background. The description of the passage from a situation to its outcome is normally expressed by an unaccomplished tense in the second member of the sentence, without necessarily stressing the future.

8. It is not my purpose here to castigate Paul for this powerful and pathetic saying, but to denounce a certain interpretation widespread among his readers.

9. In the statement of God's sabbath in Genesis 2:2, there are no less than eight words describing his activity!

10. Moses ben Maimon, *Mishne Torah, the Book of Knowledge*, V.5, 4.

11. Rollo May, *Love and Will* (New York: W. W. Norton & Co., 1969), p. 113.

12. Cf. Exodus 19:11; Joshua 1:11; Hosea 6:2; Jonah 2:1; Mark 8:2; 14:58; John 2:20; Luke 24:21. Cf. the elaboration of this idea in chapter 5 below.

13. Ernst Bloch, *Das Prinzip Hoffnung*, 2 vols. (Fankfurt: Suhrkamp, 1959), pp. 1378–1384.

14. The expression used by Max Picard in his book *Hitler in uns selbst* (Zurich: Rentsch, 1946). English translation: *Hitler in Our Selves* (Hinsdale, Ill.: Henry Regnery Co., 1947).

15. In the case of Auschwitz, as most probably in the case of Isaac (despite the Midrash), there apparently was no choice in the martyrdom. But that which is true as far as *individuals* are concerned is untrue when considered in the context of historical *Israel*. The rabbis were right in saying that Isaac "jumped on the altar" to be sacrificed.

16. Cf. Lucien Laberthonnière, *Le réalisme chrétien et l'idéalisme grec* (Paris: P. Lethielleux, 1904; reprint ed., Frankfurt am Main: Minerva Verlag, 1975), p. 105 (my translation): "this is grace, that is,

God's life continuing in the life of humanity, so that the latter can be heightened into becoming the very life of God."

Cf. Julian Morgenstern, *The Book of Genesis*, p. 52 (the author cites Psalm 8 and adds): "the goal of all human living and striving is to become even like unto God Himself. 'Ye shall be holy; for I the Lord your God am holy' (Leviticus XIX, 2), is the divinely appointed standard of human righteousness." For a discussion of this, see below.

17. Robert Martin-Achard, *Israël et les nations* (Neuchatel: Delachaux & Niestlé, 1959), p. 17 (my translation). See also Daniel 2:46; Zechariah 8:23, etc.

18. Edmond Jacob, *Theology of the Old Testament*, p. 87.

19. On this translation of the famous *"ehyeh asher ehyeh"* of Exodus 3:14 (generally and incorrectly understood after the Septuagint: "I am who I am"), see my commentary on Exodus 1—4, *Le Devenir de Dieu*. The Hebrew root *"hyh"* does not mean "to be" but "to befall, to happen." It is dynamic and indicates a historical movement of passing from one mode of being to another.

20. Jean-Paul Sartre, *The Flies*, act 2, scene 2.

21. Or the *kenosis* of God. Cf. Alexandre Safran, *La Cabale* (Paris: Payot, 1960), p. 16 (my translation): "God becomes human in humanity; the latter become God in God." "Emmanuel," God coming among us, is the outlet, the supreme fulfillment of the gift God makes of himself from the beginning. Cf. Norman Snaith, *The Distinctive Ideas of the Old Testament*, p. 58: "God was from the beginning transcendent in that He was different from man, but He was by no means transcendent in that He was remote from man. . . . Transcendence does not mean remoteness. It means otherness."

22. Gerardus van der Leeuw, "L'Anthropomorphisme comme forme de l'anthropologie," *Le Monde non-chrétien* 2 (1947):170–186 (my translation).

23. Jules Isaac dedicates his controversial book *Jesus et Israël* (Paris: Farquelle, 1949); English translation: *Jesus and Israel*, trans. Sally Grau (Holt, Rinehart and Winston, 1971) with the following words:

IN MEMORIAM
To my wife, to my daughter
Martyrs
Killed by Hitler's Nazis
Killed
Simply because their name was
ISAAC

24. See the study of the "Son of Man" in Daniel 7 in my commentary *Le Livre de Daniel* (Neuchatel: Delachaux & Niestlé, 1976); En-

glish translation: *The Book of Daniel,* trans. David Pellauer (London: SPCK, and Atlanta: John Knox Press, 1978).

25. André Neher, *Le Puits de l'exil* (Paris: Albin Michel, 1966), p. 188 (my translation).

26. Cf. Mircea Eliade, *Images et symboles* (Paris: Gallimard, 1952), chapter 1; English translation: *Images and Symbols,* trans. Philip Mairet (New York: Sheed and Ward, 1961).

27. Cf. Numbers 25:1–2; Exodus 2:20; (Rashi on) Proverbs 30:30; *Gen. R.* on Genesis 39:6 and 15:8; *Num. R.* on 9:2; *Sanh.* 70b; *Ket.* 65b.

28. Dom Emmanuel Lanne, "Notes sur la situation d'Israël par rapport aux schismes dans l'Église chrétienne," *1054–1954: L'Église et les églises* (Chêvetogne: Éditions de Chêvetogne), vol. 2, p. 80 (my translation):

    The whole of Israel's daily life, pattern of the holy history, is "sacralized" by total dependence on the living God. In Israel, culture is inseparable from religion. All the characteristics which distinguish one nation from another and which make its culture genuine were in close relationship with faith in Israel. It is therefore impossible to separate, in Israel's religion, the divine revelation from its recipient. The revelation is not enclosed in sacred books; it is first lived by a people who express their faith in sacred books dictated by God to his prophets. Israel's faith is not primarily contained in Scripture but is incarnated in the life of a people which God has chosen for that purpose.

29. Cf. my "The Hebrew Consciousness and Contemporary Man: Language as a Vehicle of Revolutionary Thought," *The Chicago Theological Seminary Register* 69 (1969).

30. Cf. Psalms 11:4; 29; 82; 89:6–8; Daniel 3:53–55 (LXX). See also Apocalypse of Moses 7:2; 17:1; Testament of Levi 3:5–8; 4:2; Ecclesiasticus 24:10. In Qumran, cf. 1 QS XI: 7–9; 1 QSa II: 8–9 (presence of the angels in the assembly of Qumran); 1 QS XI: 9–14. This element of correspondence between heavens and earth is crucial, for example, for understanding the "Son of Man" motif.

31. Genesis 11:1. True, the Biblical text refers only to a common language among people. God is not explicitly involved in the statement. The Jewish tradition, however, emphasizing the use of the term *saphah* (lip, language), instead of *lashon* (tongue) as expected, concludes that it refers to a then common ground of human dialects in God. Rashi simply says: "it is the language of the Holy."

32. Marcel Jousse, "Les Formules targoumiques du 'Pater' dans le milieu ethnique palestinien," *L'Anthropologie du geste* (Paris: Resma, 1969), p. 337 (my translation).
33. Cf. Henri Bergson, *The Two Sources of Morality and Religion*, trans. R. Ashley Audra and Cloudesley Brereton (New York: Henry Holt and Co., 1935), p. 253: "Society doubtless follows certain suggestions of inner experience when it talks of the soul; but it has made up this word, like all others, for its own convenience."
34. This is the basic meaning of the root *"dbr"* in Hebrew.
35. Edmond Jacob, *Theology of the Old Testament,* pp. 127ff. In the French, pp. 103ff.
36. Cf. Jacob Jervell, *Imago Dei. Gen 1,26f. im Spätjudentum, in der Gnosis und in den paulinischen Briefen* (Göttingen: Vandenhoeck & Ruprecht, 1960), pp. 24–51.

Chapter 5. THE MESSIANIC PEOPLE

1. *Tsedaqa*, in Hebrew a pregnant word; it is generally translated "justice" or "righteousness," but means also and *simultaneously* "innocence, faithfulness, vulnerability, *and* victory." Cf. Genesis 38:26; Psalm 7:9–10; Amos 5:24; Judges 5:11; Micah 6:5.
2. I have already touched on this question in chapter 4 above.
3. For reasons that fall in line with those I am reviewing, Luke—and only Luke—introduced another span of time between the resurrection of Christ and the beginnings of the Church.
4. *Galuth* in Hebrew has both meanings. See, for example, Isaiah 53:1 and the elaboration which follows.
5. The earliest testimony to the resurrection of Christ is found in 1 Corinthians 15:4 (written in 54, but Paul is referring to the same "gospel he preached" to the Corinthians around 50); the apostle speaks of the event having occurred "on the third day, *in accordance with the Scriptures"* (my italics; cf. also 2 Kings 20:5; Josephus, *Jewish Antiquities* VII, 280–281; VIII, 214, 218), and this does certainly indicate the rationale behind the statement. The saving acts of God occurring on a "third day" are listed, for example, in *Gen. R.* 56:1 on Genesis 22:4, "on the third day Abraham lifted up his eyes and saw the place [*maqom*]. . . ."
6. The basic idea in this mystical speculation is based on the fact that the seventh day of creation does not end, as the former ones, with the formula: "there was evening and there was morning, an Xth day." Sabbath therefore continues throughout history. But human

history is far from being the perfect rest promised by the institution of the sabbath. We are thus to expect an "eighth day" corresponding in time to the notion of the "world to come."

7. More on this in my forthcoming book on God and Auschwitz.

8. Cf. Zohar, Shemoth (see Jethro) 81*b:* "According to R. Simeon, the 'voice of the trumpet' [Exod. 20:18] is the 'word which proceedeth out of the mouth of the Lord' (Deut. VIII,3) by which 'man lives'. It is greater and stronger than all lower voices. On it depends all; it is called 'great voice', and also a 'still thin voice' (I Kings XIX, 12)." *The Zohar,* trans. Simon and Sperling, III:244–245.

9. Isaiah 42:1 and Matthew 3:17; Psalm 91:11–12 and Matthew 4:6; Isaiah 40:3 and Matthew 11:10, etc.

10. Cf. the commentary of Redaq (Rabbi David Qimchi) on Isaiah 26:9 ("the inhabitants of the world learn righteousness"): "these are the ones whose hearts God has touched and because of them does the world stand." Cf. Malachi 1:11, 14; Zephaniah 3:9–10; Isaiah 66: 19–21; Psalm 102:15.

11. Taking into account the fact that all Hebrew manuscripts of Genesis 2:4 present the anomaly that one of the consonants is written smaller than the others in the word *"lehibbar'am"* ("when they were created"), the rabbis conclude that the text can also be read through alliteration as *"le'abraham"!* It is "for Abraham" that the heavens and the earth have been called into existence.

12. Although the expression conveys a correct intuition. Cullmann speaks of the historical dialectic between "already" and "not yet," an interesting approach to the object of our discussion. Cf. Oscar Cullmann, *Christ and Time,* trans. Floyd V. Filson (Philadelphia: The Westminster Press, 1950).

13. Cf. Yves M.-J. Congar, O.P., "L'état d'Israël dans le dessein de Dieu," *Parole et mission* 2 (July 1958):172 (my translation):

In the vocabulary of the New Testament . . . *kainos* means "new," but there was in the Greek another word which also meant "new," *neos.* But the nuance between these two adjectives is very important. When one uses *neos,* there is a substitution of one person for another or of one substance for another: for example, a new property-owner. It is really another one altogether. *Per contra,* when one uses *kainos,* it is simply the renewing of the same substance, the same reality. Thus St. Paul speaks of "newness of life." There is no substitution of one subject for another, but renewal of the rules of existence. This is the expression which ought to be used when speaking of the Church vis-à-vis the Synagogue. The Church is the new People of God, not in the sense that the former has vanished and another has been brought from outside. No, it is the same People, but renewed.

14. Mark 1:24; Luke 4:34; Acts 2:27; 13:35 (cf. Ps. 16:10); 1 John 2:20; Revelation 3:7; 15:4.

15. Matthew 1:1ff.; 8:11; Luke 19:9; John 8:58; Matthew 3:4; 17:3; Mark 9:4; Luke 9:30; Matthew 19:7–9; Luke 16:29ff.; 24:27ff.; John 1:45; 3:14; 5:45–46; 7:19ff., etc. and Hebrews 8:4.

16. On all this see: (a) the earth—Exodus 19:5; Zechariah 8:23; Isaiah 66:18ff.; (b) the language—Zechariah 8:23; Isaiah 66:18ff.; Zephaniah 3:9–10; (c) the nations—*ibid.* and Hosea 2:22; Isaiah 14:1; (d) the *koshruth*—Acts 10:11–18; cf. *Mid. Tehil.* on Psalm 146:7: "in the time to come all the animals which are unclean in this world God will declare to be clean, as they were in the days before Noah. . . . in the time to come He will permit all that He has forbidden"; and (e) the concentric circles—Isaiah 42:4.

In our day the Christian exegete Gerhard von Rad (*Old Testament Theology,* trans. D. M. G. Stalker, 2 vols. [New York: Harper & Row, 1962], 1:207) says:

> on one occasion P too directs its gaze to a future in which "the glory of God will fill the whole earth" (Num. XIV.21): it therefore regards the hitherto existing limitation of Jahweh's holiness to a special cultic sphere as something temporary, which will be followed by the ultimate universalising. This idea falls into line with the oracle of one of the post-exilic prophets that "in that day" the pots in the houses and the bells on the horses' harness will be as holy as the sacred vessels in the temple (Zech. XIV.20f.), which means that then the whole realm of the secular will be taken up into Jahweh's holiness. When that happens, Jahweh's holiness will have attained its utmost goal.

17. Cf. Matthew 10:5–6; 15—24 and parallels; Acts 3:26; Romans 15:8, etc. which are so often read with skepticism in the Church.

18. Cf. Exodus 17:6; Numbers 20:8; Deuteronomy 32:13; Joel 3:18; Ezekiel 47:2; 1 Corinthians 10:4, etc.

19. Bengt Sundkler, *Contributions à l'étude de la pensée missionnaire dans le Nouveau Testament* (Uppsala: Das neutestamentliche Seminar zu Uppsala, 1937), pp. 33, 36 (my translation; Sundkler's emphasis).

20. *Ibid.,* p. 19 (my translation).

21. Quoted by Robert Martin-Achard, *Israël et les nations,* p. 71, footnote 3 (my translation).

22. Cf. *Abodah Z.* 3a; *Pessah.* 68a; *Shabb.* 88a; 137b.

Chapter 6. PAUL AND THE LAW

1. The Clementine *Homilies,* XIX.
2. Idem, *Ep. Petri,* II, 4.
3. *Ibid.,* II, 3.
4. Idem, *Recognitions,* III, 61.
5. Hans-Joachim Schoeps, *Paul,* trans. Harold Knight (Philadelphia: The Westminster Press, 1961), p. 194.
6. Edgar J. Goodspeed, *The Meaning of Ephesians* (Chicago: University of Chicago Press, 1933).
7. See Hans-Joachim Schoeps, *Paul,* p. 183 about the arguments of Paul in Galatians 3:19: "It is clear that in the heat of the contest Paul had allowed himself to be driven to make assertions which on calmer reflection he could hardly have maintained seriously, if only not to run the risk of ridicule."
8. Or, in the words of Paul Ricoeur (*The Symbolism of Evil,* pp. 142–143), "the flesh is myself alienated from itself, opposed to itself and projected outward [cf. Rom. 7:20]. . . . This powerlessness of myself, thus reflected in 'the power of sin that is in my members,' is the flesh, whose desires are contrary to those of the spirit. . . . [The flesh is not] the root of evil, but . . . the flower of evil." In the French original, p. 138.
9. Paul Ricoeur (*ibid.,* p. 129) writes: "the Pharisees . . . made observance of the Law not only an ideal limit but a practical program for living; the impossible maximum of perfection is the background for the attainable optimum of justice; nothing is demanded of a man that he cannot *do.*" Ricoeur's emphasis. In the French original, p. 125.
10. On the distinction between Torah and *"nomos"* or *"nomoi,"* cf. the Creed of the Sabbatians: " 'there will be no other Torah; *only the commandments have been abolished,* but the Torah remains binding forever and to all eternities.' " Quoted by Gershom Scholem, *The Messianic Idea in Judaism and Other Essays on Jewish Spirituality* (New York: Schocken Books, 1971), p. 157 (Scholem's emphasis).
11. Cf. *"nomos"* in *Theologisches Wörterbuch zum Neuen Testament,* ed. Gerhard Kittel, 8 vols. (Stuttgart: Kohlhammer, 1933), IV:1040 (my translation): "The rendering of Torah by *nomos* means . . . that the predominant later view of the law triumphs and achieves dominance. It also means on the other hand that the nuances of Torah, which supplement the understanding of the law in terms of teaching, instruction, and revelation, also pass over in some degree into *nomos.*" *Nomos* also appears about 200 times in the LXX, but for Paul it has become a notion "essentiellement anti-

thétique et polémique." Paul Démann, "Moïse et la loi dans la pensée de Saint Paul," *Cahiers sioniens* (Tournai, Belgium: Desclée & Co., special issue: "L'Homme de l'alliance," 1955), p. 219.

12. According to LXX Exodus 12:40, 400 years elapsed between Abraham, mentioned in Genesis 15:6, and Sinai. Paul distinguishes three eons in Israel's history, each of which is marked by a central figure: Abraham, Moses, Jesus. The common denominator binding these eras together is faith, i. e., an existential commitment independent of any performance principle. Abraham, dead in his flesh "because he was about a hundred years old," incapable of any performance, did not rely on his own strength and potency but on God's power and love (cf. Rom. 4:18ff.).

13. Dietrich Bonhoeffer, *The Cost of Discipleship* (New York: Macmillan, 1949), p. 73.

14. Claude Tresmontant, *Saint Paul and the Mystery of Christ,* p. 113.

15. Paul's ethical exhortations in each of his epistles are a clear rejoinder to the accusation of antinomianism leveled against him. David Daube has demonstrated, however, that Paul's legislation has an advisory, didactic form, stating matter-of-fact admonitions, like the French warning: *"on ne fume pas dans cette allée."* Such a form in Pauline letters "reflects the Rabbinic view of the secondary, derivative, less absolute nature of post-Biblical rules." See David Daube, *The New Testament and Rabbinic Judaism* (London: Athlone Press, 1956), pp. 90–105. The quotation is from p. 92.

16. *Psikta Rabbati* 107a: " 'Lord of the world, Thou hast too much exhorted me, until with the divine law a yoke of decrees has been placed around my neck, through which I have become guilty. Had I not received the law, I would have been as one of the heathen nations for whom there is neither recompense nor punishment.' " Quoted by Hans-Joachim Schoeps, *Paul,* p. 191.

17. Rabbi Richard Rubenstein is right in seeing Paul addressing himself, not to the very nature of Torah as such, but to the "performance principle" of those who try to accumulate the accomplishment of commandments. No one, I think, will remain indifferent to Rubenstein's confession, in *My Brother Paul* (New York: Harper & Row, 1972), pp. 7, 13:

> I was constantly confronted with the Law's basic bribe . . . : Perform well and you will be rewarded: perform badly and you will be damned. It didn't happen that way. I played the game by the rules. I did what was expected of me . . . . Nevertheless, I found that my life became increasingly distressed and anguished. . . . As long as the inclination to rebel continues, feelings of guilt and self-reproach are inevitable. . . . When this is under-

stood, it is possible to appreciate the psychological truth of one of Paul's most important insights: the fact that men can never make themselves right before God. This insight led Paul to his doctrine that God is graciously able to make just the sinner who is incapable of justifying himself.

18. *Meor Enayim* (Slavita, 1798, f. 91b), quoted by Gershom Scholem, *The Messianic Idea in Judaism and Other Essays on Jewish Spirituality,* p. 199.

19. Robert Scholes and Robert Kellogg, *The Nature of Narrative* (New York: Oxford University Press, 1966), p. 166.

20. *Ibid.*

21. George Steiner, *After Babel* (New York: Oxford University Press, 1975), p. 267.

22. Cf. Rosemary Ruether, *Faith and Fratricide: The Theological Roots of Anti-Semitism* (New York: Seabury, 1974), p. 78: "the crux of the conflict [between Christianity and the Pharisaic teachers] lay in the fact that the Church erected its messianic midrash into *a new principle of salvation."* Ruether's emphasis.

23. Cf. *ibid.,* p. 65: "the Church developed its oral New Testament upon a messianic midrash of the Psalms and Prophets." Qumran also "reads" the Bible from a point of view of its own.

24. It is remarkable that this epistle, written ca. 150, had extreme difficulties in being received into the New Testament canon. It was admitted in the fifth or sixth century.

25. *Menaḥot* 29b.

26. F. W. Beare, "Canon of the NT," *The Interpreter's Dictionary of the Bible,* 4 vols. (New York: Abingdon, 1962), 1:522.

27. That the New Testament did not originally claim to be an integral part of the record of Israel's *Heilsgeschichte* is shown by its striking silences! I mean that it saw itself excused from discussing all sorts of issues which are matters of existential concern for a historical people, such as land ownership, statehood and government, judiciary systems, social structures, political and economic doctrines, international relations, slavery, sexual standards, etc. The canonization of that midrashic document provided a solid foundation for the feeling that the New Testament's "religion" is definitely individualistic in contradistinction to Israel's historical destiny.

28. Rosemary Ruether (*Faith and Fratricide,* p. 80) shows that Christianity was not asking from Judaism any smaller sacrifice than "to abrogate itself" by substituting for its covenantal principle from the past another one supplied by Jesus. Crucially, she says (*ibid.,* p. 81), the Church insisted upon adhesion to the covenantal community "not by integrating oneself into the covenantal history of a people,

but by attaching oneself to a redemptive *figure.*" That, says Ruether, "was no problem, since this was the customary principle of initiation into the mystery religions."

29. Recall the Patristic process of disowning the Jews: the "Old Testament" was seen as having been written, as it were, in a mechanical way by a deicide, blind, and deaf nation. The institution of Christianity was presented as the first and only one to understand the message. Cf. Ruether, *ibid.,* pp. 65, 72; she writes (p. 78): "salvation was now found solely through faith in the messianic exegesis of the Church."

30. Cf. Gregory Baum, *Is the New Testament Anti-Semitic?* (Glen Rock, N. J.: Paulist Press, 1965); Dominic Crossan, "Anti-Semitism and the Gospel," *Theological Studies* 26 (1965):189–215.

31. Rosemary Ruether's argument is that the exoneration of the Romans by the Gospels goes deeper than a mere transfer of the blame to the Jews. The shift, she says (*ibid.,* pp. 88, 89), was "from *political* to *religious* authority . . . specifically upon the head of the Jewish *religious* tradition and its authority. . . . The word *Jews,* in the Gospels, Acts, and Paul, means the Jewish religious community. It is in this sense that the word *Jews* becomes a hostile symbol for all that resists and rejects the gospel."

32. The anti-Jewish polemics were not the product of the Gentile Church. But it is evident that, in passing to non-Jews, the tone and bearing of these polemics transformed what used to be a family quarrel into an open war. Not only was the original meaning of texts given new and more offensive connotations, but *the sources themselves* were tampered with by the victorious party.

33. *Gen. R., "bereshit"* VIII, 4, 5.

Chapter 7.   THE DUALITY ISRAEL-CHRISTENDOM

1. A text all the more paradoxical since it belongs to the famous chapters 9—11 on the problem of Jewish-Gentile relationships.

2. The next chapter, "Synagogue and Church," contains a discussion of the notion of "Israel *kata sarka,*" "Whole Israel," etc.

3. In the New Testament, see Acts 10:34; Romans 2:11; Galatians 2:6; Ephesians 6:9; Colossians 3:25; 1 Peter 1:17.

4. *Mekh.* on Exodus 17:6, p. 52b.

5. Georges Sorel, *Réflexions sur la violence,* 10th ed. (Paris: Marcel Rivière, 1946).

6. This unity is made manifest in the person of the child when male and female have realized their oneness. Life springs from the mutual complementation of the two poles. What is true for man

and woman is true for master and slave, black and white, Jew and Gentile, etc.

7. Cf. chapter 5, "The Messianic People."

8. Rollo May, *Love and Will*, pp. 111, 112, 113.

9. Cf. Matthew 3:2=4:17; 5:3, 10; 10:7; 11:12; John 3:3, 5; Ephesians 2:6; Colossians 2:12; 3:1, etc.

10. Martin Buber, *Ereignisse und Begegnungen* (Leipzig: Insel Verlag, 1920), p. 20 (my translation).

11. Martin Buber, *Israel and the World* (New York: Schocken Books, 1948), p. 35.

12. J. Coert Rylaarsdam, "Common Ground and Difference," *The Journal of Religion* 43 (October 1963): 269.

13. Cf. André Neher, *Le Puits de l'exil* (Paris: Albin Michel, 1966).

14. Rollo May, *Love and Will*, pp. 113–114 (May's emphasis).

15. To develop this idea from a Biblical point of view would require another study. See Erwin Reisner, *Vom Ursinn der Geschlechter* (Berlin: Lettner, 1956). Sexes in the Bible play a most important role; they are the key for understanding the relationship God-man-woman-child-animal-nature-cosmos. The sobriety of the texts when speaking of sex is to be accounted for by two factors: on the one hand, the texts embody polemics against the surrounding naturalistic, fertility-oriented religions; and on the other hand, they express the nobility, the mystery, conveyed by the meeting of two who become one (cf. "this is a great mystery, and I take it to mean Christ and the Church," Eph. 5:32, my translation; Eph. 5:21 —6:9 must be read from this perspective). The Second Epistle of St. Clement of Rome (second century C.E.) says: "Somebody asking the Lord when the Kingdom would come, he answered . . . 'When the two will be only one, when the exterior [i. e., the "convex"] will be like the interior [i. e., the "concave"], when in the encounter between male and female there will be neither male nor female.' " And the Gospel of Thomas (*The Gospel According to Thomas*, trans. A. Guillaumont et al. [New York: Harper & Brothers, 1959], logia 22 and 114, pp. 17, 19, 57) says: "They said to Him: Shall we then, being children, enter the Kingdom? Jesus said to them: When you make the two one, and when you make the inner as the outer [concave and convex in our terminology] and the outer as the inner and the above as the below, and when you make the male and the female into a single one, so that the male will not be male and the female (not) be female . . . then shall you enter [the Kingdom]. . . . Jesus said: See, I shall lead her [Mary], so that I will make her male, that she too may become a living spirit, resembling you males. For every woman who makes herself male will enter the Kingdom of Heaven."

16. Martin Buber, "Le Message hassidique," *Dieu vivant,* No. 2 (Paris: Éditions du seuil, 1945). English translation mine.

17. Cf. the Wisdom of Solomon 2:14–15: " 'He [the righteous man] became to us a reproof of our thoughts; the very sight of him is a burden to us, because his manner of life is unlike that of others, and his ways are strange.' "

18. Leo Pinsker has written: "For the living, the Jew is a dead man; for the natives, an alien and a vagrant; for the property holders, a beggar; for the poor, an exploiter and a millionaire; for patriots, a man without a country; for all classes, a hated rival." Cited by Thomas Walter Laqueur, *A History of Zionism* (New York: Holt, Rinehart and Winston, 1972), p. 72.

19. This declaration of Jesus is substantiated by quite a number of New Testament texts: cf. Matthew 2:6; 4:23; 10:5–6; 11:1; 19:28=Luke 22:30; Mark 7:27; Luke 1:16; 2:34; 9:6; Acts 3:26; 5:31; 10:36; 13:23; Romans 15:8.

20. See chapter 5 above, "The Messianic People."

21. Paul makes a deliberate mistake in his botanical metaphor: one normally grafts the cultivated olive tree onto the wild tree, not vice versa. It is clear that Paul wants to maintain the primacy of the Jews in the process.

22. In *Theologisches Wörterbuch zum Neuen Testament,* VI:869ff. (*"proton"*).

Chapter 8. SYNAGOGUE AND CHURCH

1. Franz Rosenzweig, *Stern der Erlösung,* p. 520; English translation: *The Star of Redemption,* trans. William W. Hallo (Boston: Beacon Press, 1972), pp. 415, 416.

2. Franz Rosenzweig, *The Star of Redemption,* p. 414 says: "It was always the hidden enemies of Christianity, from the Gnostics to the present day, who wanted to deprive it of its 'Old Testament.' A God who was only spirit, and no longer the Creator who gave his law to the Jews, a Christ who was only Christ and no longer Jesus, a world which was only All and its center no longer the Holy Land—... [in this kind of world] the soul would not just get lost, it would remain lost."

3. In this respect, the Gospels and epistles wholeheartedly concur. The kingdom of God and its hope "laid up ... in heaven" is "indeed in the whole world ... bearing fruit and growing ... [as it has] among yourselves, from the day you heard and understood the word of God in truth.... the Father ... has qualified you to share in the inheritance of the saints in [the kingdom of] light. He has

delivered us from the dominion of darkness and transferred us to the kingdom of his beloved Son, in whom we have redemption, the forgiveness of sins. . . . [God chose] through him to reconcile to himself all things, whether on earth or in heaven, making peace by the blood of his cross." (Col. 1:5–6, 12–14, 20; cf. 2:12–15; 3:1)

4. Søren Kierkegaard, *Angriff auf die Christenheit* (Stuttgart: A. Dorner, Chr. Schrempf, 1896), p. 95 (my translation).

5. All occurrences in the Gospels of the title "Messiah" in the mouth of Jesus are critically questionable. Probably not one of them is to be retained as authentic.

6. A. Roy Eckhardt, *Elder and Younger Brothers: The Encounter of Jews and Christians* (New York: Charles Scribner's Sons, 1967), p. 109.

7. *Ibid.*, p. 146 (emphasis mine).

8. Cf. my "The Stranger in the Old Testament," *Migration Today* 15 (1970):55–60.

9. Cf. *Sanh.* 98a; *Psiq.*, ed. Buber f. 51b.

10. Samuel Amsler, *L'Ancien Testament dans l'église* (Neuchatel: Delachaux & Niestlé, 1960), p. 114 (my translation).

11. Dom Emmanuel Lanne, *1054–1954: L'Église et les églises*, vol. 2, pp. 84–85.

12. André Neher, "Une Approche théologique et sociologique de la relation judéo-chrétienne," *Recherches et dialogues philosophiques et économiques* 96 (1959):28 (my translation).

13. Paul Démann, "Israël et l'unité de l'église," *Cahiers sioniens* 1 (March 1953).

14. Cf. Pope Pius XI: "Spiritually, we are all Semites."

15. Cf., for example, the Dogmatic Constitution on the Church (*The Documents of Vatican II*, ed. Walter M. Abbott [New York: Herder and Herder, 1966], p. 34): "Those who have not yet received the Gospel are related in various ways to the *People of God* (i. e., the Church). In the first place there is the *people* to whom the covenants and the promises were made, and from whom Christ was born according to the flesh. On account of their fathers, as regards the election, this *people* remains most dear to God, for God does not repent of the gifts he makes, nor of the calls he issues." Emphasis mine. Compare this with Franz Rosenzweig, *Briefe* (Berlin: Schocken Verlag, 1935), p. 686 (my translation): "You and I, we are inside the same borders—we are in the same kingdom."

16. According to modern historians, the historical phenomenon called anti-Semitism was initiated by Christendom. Before Christianity, there was no anti-Semitism as such. Cf. for instance, Jules Isaac's books on the matter.

17. Gutbrod, "Israel," *Theologisches Wörterbuch zum Neuen Testament,* III:370ff.
18. Cf. John 1:49 (Jesus is king of Israel; cf. 12:13); 1:31 (Jesus must be manifested to Israel); 1:47 (Nathanael is called a true Israelite); 3:10 (Nicodemus is a teacher of Israel).
19. Cf. Acts 5:21 ("neutral use"); 2:22; 3:12, 25; 13:16; cf. 4:8 if original; 2:36; 4:10; 13:24, etc.
20. I have selected this last term ("adjoined") as an attempt to describe the respective situations of Jews and Gentiles in *the* People of God. As a learned institution may be served by regular and adjunct professors, so the People of God is composed of "regular" and "adjunct" members. In practice, this means that the former are the reference of the latter, not conversely. The institution can live without adjunct teachers, but not without its faculty.
21. The RSV's translation of the passage under consideration is ambiguous because it raises a false problem: "Peace and mercy be upon all who walk by this rule, upon the Israel of God." Here it is clear that only those who "walk by this rule" (of resisting circumcision in the flesh, convinced as they are that "neither circumcision counts for anything, nor uncircumcision, but a new creation," 6:15) would be "the Israel of God."
22. During the morning service, even if it is a fasting day, this formula must be pronounced by the assembly. The pericope is introduced by the words *"sim shalom,"* and known accordingly.
23. Some texts in the Gospels, especially the parables of Jesus, seem to indicate the *replacement* of Israel *"kata sarka"* by a new people, evidently the Church. See, for example, the parable of the vineyard or the one of the great supper. In regard to the latter (Matt. 22:1–10 and Luke 14:15–24), let me stress the fact—as I already did concerning Romans 11:22–23—that the parable points to one and only one message: the room will be filled. The question is precisely *not* about the identity of the guests.

As for the parable of the wicked tenants of the vineyard (Matt. 21:33–46; Mark 12:1–12; Luke 20:9–19), we must depart from the quotation of Psalm 118:22–23 given in Matthew 21:42=Mark 12: 10–11=Luke 20:17. " 'The very stone which the builders rejected [and which] has become the head of the corner' " is the last stone put above the Temple's main door in Jerusalem. Jesus is clearly speaking of the eschatological sanctuary grounded for the purified remnant of Israel by the Messiah. The so-called "others" in the parable are thus those who belong to that *"verus Israel,"* which is not to be purely and simply confounded with the nation of Israel as a whole. The vineyard of God, Zion and Israel (cf. Isa. 5), is to become the ultimate Zion into which a great number of people will

eventually flow, not all of them expected according to the "ortho-
dox" theological previsions. For the way to that Temple not built by
human hands (cf. John 2:21; 1 Cor. 3:16, 17; 6:19; 2 Cor. 6:16; Eph.
2:21, etc.) is the one of the tortured Messiah (cf. Matt. 20:28; 21:39).

24. See David Flusser, *Jesus,* trans. Ronald Walls (New York: Herder
and Herder, 1969), p. 90: R. Nethunia the son of ha-Kanah has said,
" 'Everyone who takes the yoke of law upon him will have taken
off his shoulders the yoke of government and of daily sorrows. But
whoever puts off the yoke of the law will be burdened with the
yoke of government and of daily sorrows.' "

25. Leonhard Ragaz, *Die Botschaft vom Reiche Gottes* (1942), p. 280,
quoted and translated in David Flusser, *Jesus,* p. 89.

26. David Flusser, *Jesus,* p. 90.

27. Adolf Hitler knew this by intuition and tried to annihilate God in
the only place he could be found: in the persons of his Jews. See
my forthcoming book on God and Auschwitz.

28. Juda Halevi, *Hakuzari,* IV.23.

29. See my "The Stranger in the Old Testament," *Migration Today* 15
(1970):55–60.

30. The term *ger* therefore is in its own right a *dynamic* concept, not
just a social condition.

31. Cf. Rashi *ad loc.;* he himself refers to a Baraitha of *Sifre.*

32. It is true that the Assembly of Yamnia/Jabne added to the "18
benedictions" a curse for all *"minim"* and that the Christians were
primarily meant under this label. A ban was thus pronounced
against the heterodox—but only those who felt under criticism
excluded themselves from orthodoxy. Are *"minim"* then only
those who take themselves to be such?

33. Richard L. Rubenstein, *My Brother Paul.*

34. Cf. Samson R. Hirsch's *"Gabe ist Aufgabe"*—gift is task.

35. Cf. S. D. Goitein, *"YHWH* the Passionate: The Monotheistic Meaning and Origin of the Name *YHWH,"* Vetus Testamentum* 6 (1956):
1–9.